BILLIONAIRE DRUG LORD
JOSÉ GONZALO RODRÍGUEZ GACHA

The Untold Story of a Medellín Cartel Kingpin

MAFIA LIBRARY

© **Copyright 2024 - All rights reserved.**

The content contained within this book may not be reproduced, duplicated or transmitted without direct written permission from the author or the publisher.

Under no circumstances will any blame or legal responsibility be held against the publisher, or author, for any damages, reparation, or monetary loss due to the information contained within this book, either directly or indirectly.

Legal Notice:

This book is copyright protected. It is only for personal use. You cannot amend, distribute, sell, use, quote or paraphrase any part, or the content within this book, without the consent of the author or publisher.

Disclaimer Notice:

Please note the information contained within this document is for educational and entertainment purposes only. All effort has been executed to present accurate, up to date, reliable, complete information. No warranties of any kind are declared or implied. Readers acknowledge that the author is not engaged in the rendering of legal, financial, medical or professional advice. The content within this book has been derived from various sources. Please consult a licensed professional before attempting any techniques outlined in this book.

By reading this document, the reader agrees that under no circumstances is the author responsible for any losses, direct or indirect, that are incurred as a result of the use of the information contained within this document, including, but not limited to, errors, omissions, or inaccuracies.

TABLE OF CONTENTS

Introduction 1

Chapter 1 : The Boy Before The Drug Lord - The Early Life 5

   A Little Boy From Pacho 5

   The Family Of Farmers 8

      Father Of Gonzalo 9

      Mother Of Gonzalo 10

      Siblings Of Gonzalo 11

      Childhood Of Gonzalo 12

   Psychological And Cognitive Traits Of Gacha 14

   Gacha's Movement To Bogota 16

Chapter 2 : The Inception Of A Criminal - Criminal Origins Of José Rodríguez Gacha 17

   The Story That Started From Small Crimes 17

      Bogota And Gonzalo 17

      Initial Menial Jobs 18

      Jose Gacha's First Exposure To Small Crimes 19

      Trafficking And Illicit Trade 20

      The World Of Emerald Smuggling 20

      Green War And Its Influence On Gacha 21

      Building His Repo As Extortionist 23

Welcome To The Drug Trade 23
   The Cannabis Trade 23
   Expanding His Expertise And Cocaine Trafficking 25
   Stepping Up The Crime Game 26
   Joining Forces With Medellin Cartel 26
   Expansion Of Medellin Cartel 27
   Strategic Control Of Land And Resources 28
   Incorporation Of Threat And Aggression 29
   Ascension To The Leadership Role 30
   Connections With Notorious Names 30
   Gacha's Strategic Partnerships With Notorious Figures 31

Chapter 3 : El Mexicano - The Rise Of Power 35

   Growth And Influence Within The Cartel 35
      Militarization Of The Cartel 35
   Gacha's Terror Campaign Against The Colombian Government
   36
      Growth Of The Cultivation Area And Refining Capabilities . 37
      Gacha's Contribution To Discovering Drug Routes 37
      Gacha's Influence Within The Cartel 38
      Dive Into The International Markets 39
      Expansion Of Smuggling Networks 39
      Novelty In Supply Chain Management 40
      Advanced Money Laundering Scheme 40
      Expansion Of Medellin Cartel Into Europe 41
      Gacha's Hold Into Asian Markets 43
      Top-Down Integration And Hold On Supply Chain 43

Gonzalo Gacha's Influence On His International Ventures 44
   The Mexican Connection 46
   Spread Of Smuggling Networks 48
   Building Drug Sanctuaries In Mexico 48
   Personal Affinity With The Mexicans 49

Influence Of Ties With Mexico 50
   Provided A Base For The Rise Of Gacha As A Billionaire Drug Lord 50
   Heightened U.S. Law Enforcement Attention 51
   Becoming An International Name 51

Chapter 4 : The Foes - Law Enforcement, Rivals, And Internal Conflicts 53

Gacha Vs. Law Enforcement 53
   Bribery, Trickery, And Manipulation 54
   Combating Law Enforcement Through Aggression 55
   Targeting The Police And Military Office 56
   Deployment Of Paramilitary Personnel And Alliances 57
   Escalation Of Conflict With The Rise Of Gacha As A Drug Lord 58

Impact On Law Enforcement Strategies 59

Jose Gacha And His Rivals 60
   The Cali Cartel 61
   Fabio Ochoa Vásquez 61
   Carlos Lehder 62
   Jorge Luis Ochoa Vásquez 62
   Griselda Blanco 63

    Rafael Caro Quintero 63

    Amado Carrillo Fuentes ("El Señor De Los Cielos") 64

    Hélmer "Pacho" Herrera 64

    Victor Carranza ("The Emerald King") 64

  Gacha Vs. His Own People 65

    Rivalries From Within 66

    Internal Purges And Paranoia 67

    Rivalry With His Blood Relations, Including His Son 67

    Clashes Over The Use Of Financial Resources 68

    Impact Of Internal Rivalries 68

Chapter 5 : The End Of An Era - The Downfall Of Don Sombrero 71

  The First Crack In His Power 72

  The Constant Conflicts And Pressure 75

    Joint Efforts By Law Enforcement 75

    Failed Ventures Resulting In Financial Loss 76

    Rifts From Within The Cartels 77

    Disloyalties And Information Leaks 79

    Government's Role 80

    Scrutiny And Surveillance Efforts Of The Colombian Government 80

    Collaboration With The Dea And Cia 81

    Targeted Operations 82

    Extradition Policy And Political Pressure 82

    Public Outrage And Diplomatic Pressure 83

Crackdown Of Gacha's Network And Assets 84
    Operations Against Guerrilla Forces 84
The Final Showdown 85
    The Raid And Gacha's Death 86
    Securing The Scene 87
    Public Announcement And Media Coverage 87
    The Aftermath Of Gacha's Death 87

Chapter 6 : The After-Effects Of Rodríguez Gacha - Legacy And Impact Of His Death 89

Prompt Effect Of Gacha's Death 89
    More Aggressive Strategy Against The Government 90
    War With The Colombian Government 90
    Fragmentation Of The Cartel 91
    Rise Of Los Pepes 91
    Hard Hit To Escobar's Power And The Medellín Cartel 92
    Rise Of The Cali Cartel 93

Long-Term Impact 93

Changes In The Drug Trade 94
    Shift Of Power 94
    Decentralization Of Drug Trafficking 95
    Emergence Of New Alliances And Shifts In Drug Trafficking Routes 95
    The Role Of Nonstate Actors 96
    Technological Advancements And Drug Smuggling 96
    International Cooperation In Law Enforcement 97

Impact On Colombian Society And Politics 97

Resilience Of The Cocaine Trade 98

New Law Enforcement Strategies After Jose Gacha's Death 99

    Improved Cooperation Between Colombia And The United States 99

    Incorporation Of New Legal Frameworks And Extradition Policies 100

    Formation Of Anti-Drug Units 100

    Strengthening Of Local Law Enforcement And Intelligence Capabilities 100

    Focused Approach To Hunt Down Cali Cartel And Other Successors 101

    Shift Toward Criminal Justice Reform And Human Rights. 101

Impact On Global Drug Policy 102

    A Trendsetter For International Cooperation 102

    Shift In Focus To Cartel Leadership 102

    Development Of New Legal Frameworks And Extradition Treaties 103

    Reevaluation Of Militarized Approaches 103

    Increased Focus On Narco-Terrorism 104

    Shift Towards Alternative Development Programs 104

    Impact On Drug Policy 104

    Recognition Of The Need For Comprehensive Strategies 105

Conclusion 107

References 113

INTRODUCTION

Behind every great fortune, there is a crime.

Interestingly enough, this quote by French playwright and novelist Honore de Balzac summarizes the phenomenal life of a great Columbian drug lord. José Gonzalo Rodríguez Gacha is the name that strikes a chord with many people, who can't help but dig into the mystery built around one of the most conspicuous drug lords, a man with a legacy that his younger generations dread to follow. With crime literature primarily highlighting figures like Pablo Escobar and Griselda Blanco, the narrative of Gacha remains largely overlooked. Yet his story is equally, if not more, significant in the history of drug lords. Why did José Gonzalo Rodríguez Gacha enter the drug world? And how did he become a billionaire drug lord? Or even better, what was the impact of Jose Gonzalo Rodriguez Gacha's life on the drug world? This is the enigma that this book attempts to decode. As we prepare to explore the story of one of the most notorious figures associated with the Medellín Cartel, it is essential to understand the challenges that come with telling this gripping tale.

Gacha, also known as "El Mexicano," happens to be a founding member and one of the most important figures of the Medellin Cartel, thriving on cocaine trafficking in the 1980s, setting the trends in the global drug trade. He makes one wonder whether he should be admired for his trickery and rise from rags to riches or dreaded because of his callous end. Ambition and ruthlessness with a dash of strategical tactics are what made him one of the key figures in the war against drugs in Columbia.

This book attempts to unveil the dynamics of power warfare, the bloody war against narcotics, the violence, the crime, the politics of the drug trade, and the world of drug business.

When we talk about drug trafficking, it's a global illegal trade comprising not only the distribution, transportation, and sale of substances but also the manufacturing and cultivation of them. Drug smuggling carries severe penalties, such as the death penalty, flogging, and incarceration. There's also the fact that drug lords' connections with politicians have been disclosed in various scandals and cases.

In 2021, Interpol disclosed that drug smugglers operating in almost 90 countries were involved in selling the substance through online sources like websites. This information denotes the drug trade as one of the most violent crimes. According to a report by the U.S. Department of Justice (1994), 5% of murders happen in the U.S. due to drug-related incidents. Meanwhile, the Mexican government has announced that approximately 90% of the killings happen due to the drug trade (Shirk & Wallman, 2015). South American states like Columbia, Peru, and Bolivia are notorious for the cultivation and trade of cocaine. Criminal organizations, cartels, and local groups are involved in the transportation of drugs across the globe through complicated networks. They distribute the drugs through various methods like illegal shipping, tunnels, drones, and drug mules.

The drug trade has a long, well-documented history. Centuries ago, smugglers were involved in the transportation of opium, which was primarily used for medicinal purposes. Eventually, the Opium Wars between Britain and China due to the highly lucrative drug trade. It wasn't until the early 20th century that the drug trade of substances like opium, marijuana, and cocaine was declared illegal by the United States. During the 1970s, different strong groups (particularly the Medellin cartel,)changed the dynamics of the cocaine trade in Columbia, widening the expanse of the drug trade. In the U.S., the drug trade scenario went from being merely illegal to a "War on Drugs" (Gelber, 2006). Across the Americas, militarization and violence proliferated in the regions where the drugs were manufactured and traded. It was in this era that the emergence of drug lords like Pablo Escobar, El Chapo, Griselda Blanco, and the notorious billionaire drug lord Jose Rodriguez Gacha happened, impacting the world drug trade on a vast scale. Switching from emerald smuggling to cocaine smuggling, he was able to elevate his position in the Medellin Cartel due to clever and violent thinking. He not only expanded the trade but also militarized the operation by installing private army personnel, guerrillas, and mercenaries to protect his trade from state law. He adopted violent methods and went to the extent of attacking judges, government buildings, and anti-drug agencies to ensure a smooth drug trade.

Situations like this make the drug lord stronger yet more vulnerable at the same time. When it comes to drug mafia, drug lords, and trafficking, stories far and wide become more complicated and mysterious, igniting curiosity among all of us to learn the truth. Perhaps this book on the man known as Don Sombrero can shed light on the enigma of the global drug trade.

CHAPTER 1
THE BOY BEFORE THE DRUG LORD - THE EARLY LIFE

Before José Gonzalo Rodríguez Gacha became one of the most notorious drug lords, he had a life that is not known to many people. It's really intriguing to know what leads an innocent young boy to walk on the path of crime and become one of the most wanted criminals in American history.

Jose Rodriguez Gacha was not born with a silver spoon; in fact, it is quite surprising to find that he belonged to a family of paupers. He started off his dangerous criminal career from being a part of a humble background with meager resources and no linkage with drug lords or drug trafficking. Even his parents led a simple life, as was the case with the common farmers of that time.

A Little Boy From Pacho

Jose Gonzalo Rodriguez Gacha was born on May 14, 1947, in the small town of Veraguas, near Pacho. The town is situated in the Cundinamarca Department of Colombia. He was born and brought up in a simple, modest family of farmers. He goes by different nicknames, like Don Sobrero, meaning "Mister Hat" in English, El Mexicano, and Mexican. But who knew the little boy who was born in a land with few opportunities and practically no resources would be declared one of the world's leading billionaires by Forbes magazine after 40 years?

Pacho's origin is as recent as 1604, when it was first discovered as a colony of the Spanish government. Pachu's name was derived from its indigenous language, which is the Chibcha language. Ever since the 17th century, it has been an agricultural land relying on crops ranging from corn, beans, potatoes, and cattle farming with little room for progression and improvement in lifestyle and opportunities. This situation persisted till he came to power as a drug lord, transforming the look of the town with a mix of infrastructure development and violence as an active source of drug trade. This is a paradoxical development where some enjoyed the unprecedented availability of resources and opportunities while others faced life threats due to the new trend for militarization of the drug trade.

He belonged to a poor family of poor pig farmers in Pacho. Just like most families in the area, the Rodriguez-Gacha household depended entirely on farming for their livelihood. As was expected, his formal education ended barely beyond grade school, and he left his education well in the 1970s to pursue a career in emerald smuggling. He remained illiterate and semi-literate. Despite these limitations, his intelligence, cunning, and strategic skills to navigate his way through various trades and businesses were so refined that he changed the dynamics of the drug trade across the globe.

One can imagine that the lifestyle and the avenues for growth and personal development in a small town like Pacho were not exactly bountiful. It is situated in a valley amid the green hilly area, pretty distant from the capital of Columbia. The mountainous region hinders the possibility of advancement and better opportunities despite its mild climate. No wonder the region is known for its fertile land, which leads to enough plantation and farming activities but little room for professional growth. Even the forefathers of Gacha relied on farming, including livestock, for their source of income. With very few opportunities when it comes to quality education, Pachu had little to offer him, thus continuing the vicious circle of poverty, deprivation, and exploitation that his family had been experiencing for a number of generations. And this is something he could foresee persisting for himself and his younger generations if he didn't do anything to undo the cycle.

At that time, he had no power to bring any improvement to the town by building the infrastructure or creating business opportunities for the locals. His forefathers were farmers, and farming was his fate if he stayed in the town. But equally true is the fact that the town of his childhood was a quiet and peaceful town away from the hustle and bustle of the city life of Bogota.

Growing up in a rural setting with fewer opportunities and resources, Gacha felt suffocated. Tired of the constant economic and financial challenges, he wanted to leave his hometown and build a different life for himself—one where he didn't have to be at the bottom. Throughout history, tough socio-economic conditions like these have brought out either the best or the worst in individuals. On the one hand, there are people who used these hardships as a springboard to becoming productive members of society, not to mention humans with high character. Through hard work and an emphasis on integrity, these people rose above their difficult environment and created new opportunities for themselves and others. On the other hand, there are people like him who unleashed their vindictive side in an effort to get ahead in life. Opting for underhanded tactics rather than strategies on the up and up, these people amplified the negativity of their harsh conditions. Despite accumulating wealth and power, they ended up perpetuating the cycle of inequality in their respective communities and societies.

Gacha could perceive quite clearly that staying in the town meant only one thing, which was to rely on farming and stock rearing as a source of income. It was a place that had been a farming land since 1604, and no miracle was going to happen soon to turn his life. If he wanted to change his fate for a better lifestyle and resources, he better buckle up and take the first step of leaving the town, only to return there accomplished, equipped with the power to bring change. He changed the dynamics of the town entirely during his power till his death in 1989; whether he changed the place for the good or the bad is still a question. His childhood struggles were a huge mirror into the upcoming years of his life, as his big ambitions and dreams wouldn't make him stop at anything.

The Family of Farmers

José de Jesús Rodríguez Vargas was the father of José Gonzalo Rodríguez Gacha. Like many other men in his area, his father was also involved in agriculture. He used farming and manual labor as the primary source of bread and butter for his family. Despite the fact that young Gonzalo loathed his poor lifestyle, he still inherited the strong work ethic that his father had. He saw his father work hard day and night, but no matter how hard he worked, it was never enough to overcome their financial challenges. That was because of the traditional setup of the Pachu, which could not go beyond the status of an agricultural country even after the struggle of three centuries. That's when Gonzalo realized that it was important to put in the hard work where it mattered.

Father of Gonzalo

The father of Gonzalo was Jose de Jesus Rodriquez Vera, who was a small-scale peasant farmer and livestock keeper in Pachu. Just like other families in the town, his father cultivated crops to support his family financially. His father labored for plenty of hours to produce a better yield for the crop but with little success. All he could manage was to produce enough to make both ends meet, which is one of the reasons he could not afford a quality education for his son Gonzalo. According to one analysis, Gonzalo inherited the quality of hard work and never giving up from his father, who was old school and a devout follower of the Catholic Church. One interesting fact about the town of Pachu is that there were instances of gold, emeralds, and trade of other expensive materials, creating room for smuggling or illegal trade in the town. The emerald smuggling in the town became the first premise for Gonzalo to pursue a career in smuggling.

The most conspicuous thing to remember while passing judgment on Gonzalo's life choices is the challenges and issues that his father faced for being an honest and hardworking farmer of the town with little reward. He could neither bring comfort to his family nor could he improve the lifestyle of his children, failing to provide them a basic need such as a quality education, which resulted in Gacha barely studying beyond high school. In fact, not only was his family affected by a lack of resources, but the people of the whole town also met the same fate. The most prevalent challenges included no direct access to the market, which made the prices of the crops unpredictable. Worse still, the crops were at the mercy of weather conditions like storms, floods and droughts.

The financial constraints and the economic challenges of the town during Gonzalo's childhood played an important role in making him realize that, if he wanted to succeed in acquiring wealth, he would have to leave traditional and fair means. While there was no direct influence from José de Jesús Rodríguez Vera on Gonzalo in terms of adopting drug smuggling as a professional, the poverty and misery of his family intrigued Gonzalo enough to put an end to this misery and harsh circumstances. A little reward for the hard work of his father and no chance for social mobility led him to make such a challenging decision. It is important to understand that, with no background support and precedent, ventures like emerald smuggling and then later on the drug trade required a hell of a lot of mettle, determination, hard work, and diligence to be successful in it.

Mother of Gonzalo

Gonzalo's mother, Rosa Amelia Gacha Carrillo, was the one who kept the family and their home together. Interestingly, she was like Gonzalo's father, who was also a peasant. She was a plain woman, and her life revolved around her family, traditional and religious beliefs, and the agricultural profession. As a mother and partner of her husband, she was a simpleton just like her husband and dedicated to serving the people in her household. She was the center of her home, making sure to meet the expectations of her family. She supported her husband however she could and was the anchor of the family during rough times. She nurtured her children and taught them the importance of resilience in life. Just like any other mother, she instilled values such as hard work, determination, and discipline to combat the tough circumstances. Although his mother never revealed the traits of trickery and deceit, nor did she teach Gonzalo anything of the sort, it was her upbringing that made Gonzalo strong and determined enough to come out of the hole of poverty and misery and fight the battle for his self-betterment.

Siblings of Gonzalo

The siblings of Gonzalo lived private lives with no connection whatsoever to either the drug trade or Gonzalo's business ventures in the town per se. This is one of the reasons why the exact number of Gonzalo's siblings is still unknown. This also establishes his ventures like emerald smuggling and the drug trade as purely his personal endeavors, and his family, including his parents and siblings, had no role in providing him the precedent or even moral or financial support. Although there is just a little information available on the siblings, here is what is known regarding Gonzalo's siblings:

Juan Fernando Rodriguez Gacha

One of the Gacha brothers is Juan Fernando Rodriguez Gacha, who had always lived a life of anonymity and layman. He had little involvement in whatever was going on in Gonzalo's life of notoriety and the drug trade world, whether in the early stage of their struggles or later on when Gonzalo had established himself as a public figure, though a controversial one. He had more of a reputation for staying connected with the family's business dealings. Interestingly, Gonzalo handled some of the businesses. But one thing is sure: His brother led a life of a layman and simplicity.

Felipe Rodriguez Gacha

His other brother, Felipe, is also known to have led a life of anonymity and little public exposure. He had little connection with the illicit drug dealings of Gonzalo and his life of infamy and scandal. Just like Juan Fernando Rodriguez Gacha, he had a role in handling the family business, a few of which were handled by Gonzalo too. This is not to say that he was active in the illicit drug trade and the violence that proliferated as Gonzalo's hold on the drug trade across the globe was established.

Likewise, his other siblings were simple people living a life of deprivation, quietude, and anonymity, but after the emergence of Gonzalo as a drug lord, they had their share in the sufferings that followed the notoriety and violence of his career. The family faces issues ranging from scrutiny, stigma, and the threat of attacks looming large in their lives, especially after the death of Gonzalo in 1989. The pressure and threats were from the police as well as the rival drug dealers. Certain reports verify that they were forced to leave their town to escape the potential attacks on their lives due to their association with Gonzalo.

Childhood of Gonzalo

Gonzalo, though known to have been born into a poor and humble family of peasants, exhibited signs of ambition and rebellion that reflected well into his later life of infamy as a drug lord. His rebelliousness translated into his behavior as a student. In school, he had a reputation for being unruly and over-ambitious. Like other men of extraordinary qualities who were the kings of their fates, he found school to be a prison, the job of which was to stifle the abilities of the students by providing a restrictive and confining learning environment.

There have been reported incidents of Gonzalo clashing with his teachers and his classmates. He has been known to have an aggressive temperament and little tolerance for injustice happening around him. Also, he never appreciated being confined to a certain set of rules unnecessarily. He believed that the implementation of rules had just one goal, which was to kill willpower, individuality, and ambition to excel. Eventually, due to his dissatisfaction with the school system and burgeoning sense of deprivation, limited opportunities, and poverty, he left formal education to find better opportunities and to support his family financially. It is quite interesting to note that, despite not acquiring a formal education, he was well-equipped with IQ and the required set of skills to not only thrive in the global drug trade but also to transform the dynamics of the market by introducing militarization for security purposes.

However, things were not as easy and smooth as they sound now; after dropping out of school, he did a couple of jobs to earn income, including working as a laborer. It was quite an eye-opening revelation that, after hours and hours of hard work, he was paid meagerly. This was the period when he, for the first time, encountered pinching ground realities and his laid-out destiny to live a life of deprivation and poverty. He could envision his later generation burning in the same misery. This was also the time when the cruel realities of his life in terms of land disputes and social inequalities dawned upon him, and he had no window open to escape. This period of his life, when he came in close proximity to violence, conflict on land ownership, and hardships, had a great impact on his psyche, transforming him into a ruthless, unruly, and formidable drug lord.

Ever since he was a child, he was completely aware of his poor lifestyle and lack of opportunities around him, unlike many others. While the other people of his region had accepted their living conditions, Gacha was continuously bothered by the harsh realities of poverty. Lack of education and economic growth in the region was also a prominent contributor to igniting his fire to do and get more, by hook or by crook. At this point, the only thing that young boy wanted was to escape the prison of poverty and find the fastest and most efficient path to wealth and influence.

Psychological and Cognitive Traits of Gacha

He was equipped with the traits of overambition and ruthlessness; he could go to any extent to achieve his goals. It was this intimidating personality that attracted the attention of leading drug lords even when he was quite new to it. They could see a potential ally in him for being not only a merciless but also a resourceful person. In a way, the key figures of this time saw themselves in him; like them, he would stop at nothing to get what he wanted. Though this trait clearly established common ground, it also meant that Gacha could one day supplant them as *the* kingpin of the drug trade.

His second trait was strategic thinking skills. He had one hell of a cunning mind to turn the events in his favor before you even knew it. His strategic thinking enabled him to stay several steps ahead in the game. This is something that is in high demand in the world of smuggling and drug trafficking. Later on in life, he would encounter adversaries that warranted the full use of his strategic mind. Of course, any individual going up against government forces has to prove their mettle in terms of crafting and executing intricate plans. On top of this, a person who is dealing with rival organizations left and right also has to wield instruments of mental warfare while also employing a plethora of defensive tactics for self-preservation. With his apparent predisposition to cerebral supremacy, proved to be cognitively and psychologically ready for these future challenges.

The third trait that came in handy in the world of drug trafficking in no time was his knack for violence and formidability. Even when he was quite young, well into his teens, he demonstrated his knack for violence to achieve his goals. The absence of reluctance or hesitation to remove any hurdle in whatever shape it appeared made him invincible in the world of drug smuggling. It does take a certain depth of character to silence any semblance of conscience and engage in brutality without a figment of remorse. This trait goes beyond desperation to improve one's lot in life; it indicates a callousness that makes a person indifferent to all else other than the attainment of one's goals.

The fourth trait was his obsession with wealth and unlimited power. His dream of rising higher beyond the meager means of his current life caused him to leave school and menial labor, then join the trade of emerald smuggling afterwards. With his willpower and fearlessness, he wanted to break the shackles of misery. In this case, the quote "Money can't buy happiness" has no significance whatsoever. From an early age, he had his eyes set on accumulating tremendous amounts of wealth, which was essentially the opposite of the life he'd been used to. In addition, he dreamed of becoming immensely influential so that he could bend other people to his will and wield a vast network to make himself even wealthier.

It was the willpower to break free from the fate that had befallen the locals of Pacho that led him to join the world of crime. The world of crime was apparently his only option, and he realized this quite soon. One proof of this is that, right after leaving school, he tried to work as a laborer and did a couple of menial jobs, but then, he saw the life of his own father repeating in front of his eyes: exhausting hard work with little reward to make both ends meet. It was then that he left the laborer's job and began working as a bodyguard for a local trafficker. This was his first exposure to the world of illegal business dealings, violence, and orchestrated crime world. It was then that his strategic thinking came in handy when he developed a vast network of contacts and a reputation for being a ruthless, formidable, and cunning dealer.

In short, even a family itself doesn't know what a sea of qualities and strengths a man can hold inside unless an opportunity strikes. Sometimes, this sea of qualities implores a person to come out of the box and dive into an opportunity to extract the best in store for him. The best sometimes lies intact in the storage, but in other instances, just like in the case of Gonzalo, it has to be snatched or extracted and made a part of his fate.

Gacha's Movement to Bogota

When he was still a teenager, he found a way to move to the city of Bogotá, where his only purpose was to build a better life for himself and improve his lifestyle. In the beginning, he earned little money despite tirelessly working in various odd jobs, such as construction worker and driver. The more he lived and worked in the urban areas, the more he found himself exposed to the hidden realities of the city. The prospect of his father's life (one of meaningless struggle) playing right in front of his eyes dreaded him to the core.

He was observant of the activities of street gangs and criminal networks and how they took place. This life that he saw in front of his eyes seemed so different from the one that he had led all his life. He was attracted to try something new, and that was when he took his first few steps into the world of crime by participating in a few illicit activities and forming connections with these people.

CHAPTER 2
THE INCEPTION OF A CRIMINAL - CRIMINAL ORIGINS OF JOSÉ RODRÍGUEZ GACHA

The Story That Started From Small Crimes

The young Rodríguez Gacha, with dreams in his eyes, left school as he owned a rebellious and aggressive nature. Compliance was not what he could ever acquire; perhaps he was not built to embody obedience, patience, tolerance of meager opportunities, constant poverty, and a sense of deprivation. Staying in the town of Pacho made him feel stuck to his father's miserable fate. His circumstances were in sharp contrast to his temperament, which included ambition, insubordination, and ruthlessness. Refusing to give in to the flawed system on the one hand and being forced to earn a few bucks to support his family on the other hand, he quit school. Even at that time, he did not have the intention to join the world of crimes and smuggling. This is reflected in his first appointments as a laborer in the menial jobs.

Bogota and Gonzalo

As soon as he left formal education, he found no source of employment in the town of Pacho. Because of this, he moved out of town. What place could be better than the capital city of Columbia in terms of opportunities, trade, and economic stability? At the time, it was a transitioning period for significant social and economic growth in Bogota. Urbanization and modernization were on the rise, with scattered traces of political unrest in the capital city (Tellez, 2018).

As a matter of fact, he was not alone in turning towards Bogota to seek better opportunities and turn his fate from poverty to betterment. There was a common trend among Colombian citizens living in rural places to migrate to urban cities like Bogota to escape poverty. Bogota itself was not quite ready to accept the exodus of the rural population and started expanding beyond the boundaries defined in the colonial era. The growing population due to rural-urban migration was accommodated in the fringes of the city, incorporating the suburbs into the city haphazardly.

Initial Menial Jobs

Gonzalo Gacha was one of many migrating aspirants who had left their native cities to start their life afresh in the capital city of Bogotá, where his only purpose was to build a better life for himself and improve his lifestyle. In the beginning, he earned little money despite tirelessly working in various odd jobs, such as construction worker and driver. It is quite evident when Gonzalo left school that his intentions were quite clear and simple: to live a better life with facilities and luxuries, not necessarily to infiltrate the world of organized crime. Little did he know that, in the near future, he would become a drug lord, changing the dynamics of the world of crime and drug trafficking by transforming it through militarization and mafia.

His first menial job was being a farm laborer in Pacho. His main jobs included petty jobs like planting, harvesting, and keeping an eye on the crops. Though this appeared to be an unrelated job to his later role as a drug lord, he acquired basic knowledge about farming, which he could apply to his dealings with the coca growers.

His other menial job as a laborer was in the emerald mines of the Boyaca region. This experience introduced him to an entirely different world of violence, conflicts, and control over emeralds. It was his first exposure to the illegal workings of the mines and the illicit trade for emeralds, which involved killings and lootings. His main jobs included manual jobs like digging, sorting, and even taking care of the transportation of the precious stones. However, it provided him with an opportunity to get firsthand experience of how the mining business works and how the smugglers and criminals involved in the emerald illegal trade go about their operations.

Hence, his intentions when he left the school were to find means, any means, to reach a better status and bring fortune to his family, which was already struggling with meager resources. In this sense, just about anyone could empathize with him, a boy who wanted to live an improved quality of life and explore the world beyond the confines of his locale. After all, people can easily relate to an individual striving to defy the limitations of their social environment. What set Gacha apart from other ambitious human beings was his cold, calculating mind and his propensity for savage solutions.

Jose Gacha's First Exposure to Small Crimes

It is quite dramatic how Gonzalo's first exposure to the crime world was through his work as a laborer in the emerald mines. This environment gave him a glimpse of opportunities for financial growth as well as the dynamics of power politics among drug lords. Following were some of the initial small crimes that he committed on route to the destined world of crime, power, and luxury:

Trafficking and Illicit Trade

His earliest minor crimes included bootlegging and trafficking of alcoholic drinks, such as whisky. He also started the illicit trade of contraband cigarettes in other regions and observed an acute demand for the products. He had not strengthened his grip on the world of smuggling and bootlegging yet, which is why the scope of the illegal trade of alcohol and cigarettes was quite limited. Although the scale of initial smuggling was quite small, it made him learn quite a lot about the dynamics of the smuggling world. This was the period when he started building strong connections with the formidable but corrupt officials in the government as well as the military, which came in handy later on as he built on his drug trafficking network. This period is also marked by his first exposure to the legalities of the trade and how law enforcement agencies checked the discrepancies in the smuggling and bootlegging trade. It would not be wrong to say that, if he had not started small crimes, things would have been quite different in his life.

The World of Emerald Smuggling

He started off as a laborer in the emerald mines, but there is no evidence that suggests that he took the job as a laborer in the mines to get an entrance into the world of organized crime. But his first job in the mines revealed that the emerald trade was quite prosperous and profitable trade in the town, which was hogged by the towering smugglers in the Columbia. It was still the 1970s, and he was quite a young man, barely in his 20s, struggling to seek better opportunities and equally disappointed with the state of affairs that existed at that time. Fortunately for Gonzalo Gacha (and unfortunately for law enforcement agencies), the 1970s was an era marked by the "Green War." This was the war going on in the Boyaca region among the emerald traders, who sought to acquire absolute control over the emerald mines and the trading dynamics.

Green War and Its Influence on Gacha

Apparently, the "Green War" (also known as Guerra Verde) had nothing to do with what was to follow in Gonzalo Gacha's future life (Brazeal, 2014). But it gave an unprecedented exposure to the world of crimes, where emerald traders had daggers drawn at one another. The Green War basically refers to the historic conflict that engulfed the region of Boyaca due to emerald mining. The intensity of the conflict was quite high in the towns of Coscuez, Muzo, and Chivor because these towns had been home to quite rich sources of emerald reservoirs. The emeralds themselves held quite a high value financially, leading to violent clashes among emerald traders to maintain and expand their hold in the emerald mines and the subsequent trade. Quite interestingly, the clashes brought various factions into its hold, including local miners, paramilitary groups, emerald dealers, private businessmen, and even drug cartels.

There could not have been better timing, as just when the Green War was happening, Gonzalo Gacha worked as a miner. This work exposed him to the politics and violence of the emerald world, bringing out his innate qualities of trickery, violence, formidability, and willpower to survive the world of organized crime. This experience also helped him understand the position of the government and law enforcement agencies vis-à-vis local miners and traders, as the conflicts originated partly from a fight to hold dominance over mines, ensuring wealth and control among the local dealers, landowners, and criminal organizations; and partially due to the inability of the government and law enforcement to maintain law and order in the situation.

It was a clash among the fighting factions to establish the upper hand over the emerald trade, but it also involved paramilitary forces financing and actively participating to make it more intense and bloody. Moreover, criminal organizations like drug cartels also got involved in the clashes as they also started investing their profits into the industry for more wealth or to turn their black money into white. The simple trade transformed into money laundering and narcotics trafficking with the involvement of paramilitary forces and the drug cartels as they provided finance as well as security guards to the emerald traders, intensifying the situation even further.

As a consequence of the involvement of drug cartels, the clashes naturally turned violent with the incidents of murders, assassinations, kidnappings, and extortion. The region became a red zone for causing collateral damage and general lawlessness. The conflicts lasted till the 1980s, when the efforts of the Colombian government achieved some sort of order with the help of peace treaties among various warring factions, as well as the regulation of the emerald trade. But by that time, he had gained his grip on drug smuggling and bootlegging.

The Green War holds an important place not only in the crime-filled history of Columbia but also in the life of Gonzalo, who is the offspring of the clashes and conflicts that occurred during the war. One may wonder how the Green War became a cause of his rise as a drug lord. This could be explained by the fact that it was at this time that he began as a small-time player by providing security to conflicting factions by hiring gunmen and engaging in the protection rackets. This also led to another hallmark in his career as a drug lord: He built plenty of contacts with other formidable criminals, learning how to get things done through bribery and violence.

Building His Repo as Extortionist

His initial crime acts also included the conduct of robberies and extortions, as he demanded charges for protection from local businessmen and merchants in order to establish his image as an intimidating figure in the area. This established his reputation as a formidable person who became an attraction for the prevalent drug lords to incorporate him for their protection. His ruthlessness and lack of hesitation to use violence to achieve his goals put him in high demand by the drug lords. His initial impression as a cruel, fearless, and invincible criminal allowed him to establish a strong foothold in the world of organized crimes strongly, so much so that he was sought after to provide protection personnel to the leading drug lords of that time.

Welcome To The Drug Trade

The career of Jose Gonzalo Rodriguez Gacha as a drug smuggler began with the illegal trade of marijuana because, after years of struggle as a menial worker, he realized that his fate would not change as long as he remained a menial laborer. He had gained a bit of experience working with smugglers, criminals, and illegal traders while also dealing with emerald miners and businessmen.

The Cannabis Trade

Before he emerged as a drug lord dealing with high-risk and more expensive drugs like cocaine, he smuggled less important drugs like marijuana on a small scale as his initial ventures. Although dealing with marijuana smuggling was a minor crime and therefore less risky, the opportunity equipped him with the skills to tackle tricky situations in drug trafficking operations, which were to be carried out later on. The tricks he learned during the illegal marijuana trade included how to evade authorities, establish and maintain secret but secure transport routes, and handle smugglers and distributors tactfully to establish dominance.

He used to transport marijuana from the Colombian Caribbean coast to other areas of the country and sometimes across the border. He picked up marijuana to trade illegally because of a couple of reasons. First of all, the increasing demand for Colombian marijuana across the U.S. was due to the ongoing cultural movements. Taking advantage of the opportunity for increased demand, he started the illegal trade of the drug, but the canvas of his trade was still small and limited in operation. But it was a significant period for him to learn the tricks for handling contraband over difficult areas and even across borders; these tricks would come into play in the future when he embarked on his most dramatic role as a drug lord of lucrative and risky cocaine smuggling.

This period also enabled him to develop a network of contacts in the world of smuggling, crime, and violence. He also built connections with growers of marijuana, the transporters of the drug, and the corrupt officials who played a significant role in making the process of smuggling smooth and convenient. What is more interesting is that he not only built on the network that grew with his connections and contacts, but he also emerged as a valuable asset to the existing drug lords due to his streak of violence, ruthlessness, and trickery. The point is quite pertinent here because he gained a reputation for getting through law enforcement and shipping contents safely to the destination.

Although the marijuana trade is not considered a lucrative one in comparison to the cocaine trade, he was smart enough to collect the wealth in a fair amount. He did not waste his earnings from the marijuana trade on useless activities and luxuries; instead, he invested these earnings to expand his domain and dominance in the world of smuggling by broadening his networks.

Gonzalo entered the crime world through small crimes that could enable him to make some quick cash. It was smuggling that marked the beginning of the incursion into the sphere of criminality. At the end of the 1960s and the beginning of the 1970s, Colombia was one of the world centers of various illicit businesses, and smuggling was the path to success for young and daring people like Gonzalo. He began by smuggling assorted commodities, including alcohol and cigarettes, from Colombia to other countries. This did not take long because his skills in the trade were quickly branded as resourceful, and this saw him move to another lucrative business of compounding his unlawful activities.

Expanding His Expertise and Cocaine Trafficking

It would not be wrong to call him an opportunist because, when marijuana was in high demand, he took advantage of the situation and started the illicit trade of the drug across various states of the U.S. Likewise, when the demand for cocaine increased in the mid-1970s, he did not back off but rather jumped in to make full use of the available opportunity. It was at this point that his savings from the marijuana trade came in handy as he invested those to expand his network for smuggling and get involved in trades for more expensive drugs like cocaine. As a visionary drug lord, he could foresee the bright future and the monetary benefits of investing in the illegal trade of cocaine. As luck would have it, Columbia was (and still is) the home for the best quality production of cocaine. Being a leading producer of the drug, it automatically became a hub for the processing and distribution of the drug across the border or even within various states of the U.S. Seeing a bright future in cocaine smuggling, he immediately joined the other criminal groups and organizations that were involved in the cocaine business.

Stepping Up the Crime Game

The nickname "El Mexicano" was given to Rodríguez Gacha because of his love for the Mexican style and the respect of Mexican bandits and drug dealers. This fascination not only led to the adoption of the nickname "Bone Crusher" but also encapsulated his style of constructing his criminal empire. When it comes to career progression in the field of drug trafficking, the man who stands out as a uniquely strategic thinker and is also best known for introducing such brilliant moves as the creation of direct supply lines from Colombia to the U.S. and the forging of powerful associations with Mexican drug cartels.

Joining Forces With Medellin Cartel

As soon as Gonzalo Gacha expanded his network and joined the cocaine trade as one of the leading forces in the criminal world, he took his first step into the organized world of crime. One could call it a coincidence that, just when he joined the world of cocaine smuggling, there was a criminal enterprise still in its beginnings led by the great drug lords of the period. He joined the alliance of traffickers, coming in close connection with great figures in the world of crime and illicit trade like Pablo Escobar, Carlos Lehder, and the Ochoa brothers. It was a great forum for him to learn from the ruling drug lords of the period as he gained an advantage from the current positions of the founders of the Medellin Cartel, who proved beneficial for him. For example, he made his political connections through his interactions with Escobar, who was quite a resourceful person in this regard. Lehder helped him polish his smuggling skills by learning logistic innovations. The world of organized crime also demands one to have strong connections with fellow members of illicit trade as well as to hold a good position to influence the family network. In this regard, the Ochoa brothers proved to be of great help to him. He became popular and well-connected in no time.

The credit for creating his space in the world of organized crimes does not entirely go to the Medellin Cartel, as it was also his innate abilities that led him to the path of goal achievement and notoriety. In no time, he proved himself to be a valuable asset to Medellin Cartel through the display of his administrative efficacy skills, his popularity for callousness, and the introduction of the latest techniques for conducting drug smuggling. On top of all that, his retrospective knowledge of the dynamics of farming (which he had plenty of, since he had already served as a farmer during his period of struggle) also streamlined the functioning of the organization. His understanding of the geographical terrain of the trafficking route for the trade and his expertise in transporting illegal commodities elevated the Medellin Cartel as an influential organization. He organized the transportation route of the cocaine from the Andean lab to the Caribbean and other regions, making it more secure and safe, evading law enforcement and attacks from rival groups. He made the Medellin Cartel formidable as an organization by introducing violence to safeguard the interests of the organization and its members against law enforcement as well as rival traders.

Expansion of Medellin Cartel

Though Gacha joined the organization when it was already being handled by leading drug lords, it was still in its infancy. In no time, he found his place as an important and leading member of the enterprise through his display of a unique set of skills and qualities, which he maximized to take the organization beyond just conducting operations of smuggling. He initiated the involvement of the members every step of the way until the smuggling of the final product, which was cocaine. He even took care of the production of cocaine since he had skills as a farming laborer, and he understood the dynamics and nuances of the farming processes involved in the production of cocaine. He also ensured that the cocaine's raw material was processed in hidden laboratories under their supervision to avoid any kind of digressions. Through experience in emerald smuggling, he was already familiar with the safe routes for transportation and distribution of the drug to the final destination, which was either Mexico or the United States. Instead of merely focusing on transportation logistics, he increased his wealth by handling the entire supply chain, from production and processing to the transportation and distribution of the drug.

This draws attention to two indispensable qualities: his attention to detail and his hands-on approach. Having been immersed in logistics and production (by way of the menial jobs that he took on early in his career), he understood the intricacies of procuring and distributing products for optimal profit. Aside from his knowledge of what it takes to get from point A to point B across various operations, he was also aware that he had to safeguard each step in his production chain. A single setback (whether in the manufacturing or transportation of a product) could have huge financial implications, and Gacha would have none of that, hence the hands-on style in terms of managing the supply chain.

Strategic Control of Land and Resources

The credit for acquiring a vast expanse of fertile land for producing cocaine goes entirely to Gonzalo Gacha as he ensured that the land to be farmed for drug plants should be located in remote areas to evade law enforcement and political involvement. To further secure the process of the illicit trade, he set up clandestine laboratories that were used to process the cocaine. This not only secured the drug from being captured by government officials to control the trade but also made it cost-effective, increasing the profit manifold.

Before expanding his wealth and influence, he saved his earnings from the early trade of marijuana to invest in properties across Colombia. He included farms, laboratories, ranches, and businesses to multiply his profits and wealth. No wonder that, in a matter of years, he emerged as a leading billionaire drug lord with huge influence in politics as well as the trade world. This strategic approach to the cocaine trade enabled him to hold a dominant position over strategic areas that were held quite crucial for the drug trade, diversifying his income and dominance. The unprecedented expansion of his network for the drug trade put plenty at unease, but he knew his game quite well. He won the favor of the local authorities and the other criminal groups through bribery, thus expanding his already vast kingdom of the trade network. He went to the extent of hiring private bodyguards and militia to secure his routes, farms, and laboratories effectively. This last point is quite noteworthy because the incorporation of private militia for protection was quite a novel idea in the world of organized crime in the 1970s.

Incorporation of Threat and Aggression

One of the major survival techniques used in order to establish his control over the criminal world was his knack for using violence in the name of self-protection. It makes one wonder that he belonged to a common and humble family with no background of aggression. He would not hesitate for even a moment before resorting to violence just to achieve his targets. He was responsible for the organized assassinations of rival groups, competitors, or even alleged traitors. Due to his aggression and violent techniques, he became one of the essential members of the hierarchy of the Medellin Cartel. In no time, he gained respect and popularity in the world of organized crime because of his brutality, massacre, and intimidating image within his network. Even rivals feared crossing paths with him, as he wasted no time eliminating whatever hurdle came his way.

Ascension to the Leadership Role

He joined the Medellin Cartel in the mid-1970s, and that is when he started the cocaine trade, gradually expanding his territory and influence. In less than a decade, he had ascended to the leadership role of the Medellin Cartel. Through his ability to expand the network of the enterprise by forging alliances, stretching terrain for the operations, and eliminating potential dangers by building an intimidating image, he made himself indispensable to the Medellin Cartel's operations. He introduced the use of innovative and effective strategies, including novel smuggling routes, incorporation of semi-submersibles and air transportation, and use of the hidden sections within the vehicles to evade law enforcement and government officials during the cocaine transport. He changed the nuances of the drug trade by unprecedented glorification of the violence and bloodshed in the world of crime and drug trade. He exemplified the manipulation of the Colombian drug trade during the cocaine trade boom, leaving the imprint of being the most feared criminal in the history of the drug trade.

Connections With Notorious Names

Considering the risk and the rising restrictions on the drug trade by law enforcement and government officials, Gonzalo knew that he could not survive alone in the world of organized crime. To make his footing strong, he joined a budding enterprise of criminal activities, which was being led by the leading drug lords during the 1960s and 1970s. Through the Medellin Cartel, he came in close proximity to the notorious criminals of Colombia; this allowed him to expand his skill set while also creating a platform to show off his abilities.

Gacha's Strategic Partnerships With Notorious Figures

His partnership with the notorious drug lords of the underworld led him to his current position as a billionaire drug lord.

Alliance With Pablo Escobar

Gacha was quite impressed with the charismatic and ambitious personality of Pablo Escobar, who was at that time the leader of Medellin Cartel. Through his influential and impressive personality, Escobar was able to establish and maintain control of the Medellin Cartel in the world of drug smuggling and related organized crimes. However, the alliance was not one-sided but rather a mutual one, as Escobar was equally impressed with him for his violent and aggressive nature, which not only safeguarded the operation of Medellin Cartel but also presented an intimidating image of the enterprise. In collaboration, they lifted the status of the Medellin Cartel from a lowly organization to a force to be reckoned with. In this era, the corporation saw improvements in the transportation of drug routes as well as enhanced profits, solidifying the place of the Medellin Cartel in the region. Besides that, investment in the stretch of suburban land to grow cocaine also enabled him to become a valuable asset to the enterprise.

Partnership With the Ochoa Brothers

The founding members of Medellin Cartel were the Ochoa brothers: Jorge Luis, Juan David, and Fabio. They accepted a novice like into the drug trade not out of goodwill alone. The partnership occurred due to the extraordinary qualities of Gacha, which became popular in the criminal world in a short time. He also took advantage of the partnership since the brothers were Colombian natives with roots in Colombian society, helping them establish a strong and deep-rooted hold over the politicians and legal administration. It was through the help of corrupt government officials and legal aid that the Medellin Cartel was protected and successfully executed. Being an efficient and advanced smuggler, established contacts with law enforcement and politicians with the help of the Ochoa brothers. Gacha could use inaccessible distribution routes for operations through their contacts in not only the U.S. but also Europe, thus expanding his influence. On the other hand, the Ochoa brothers made use of paramilitary forces provided by him to help them protect and successfully execute their operations for smuggling.

Collaboration With Carlos Lehder

Another strong connection built due to membership in the Medellin Cartel was with Carlos Lehder. He was the first drug lord to introduce the use of air transport for smuggling cocaine via direct access to the U.S. With his latest techniques for drug smuggling gaining plenty of traction, Gacha struck a partnership with him. He also knew that Lehder held a strong hold on the Island of Norman's Cay in the Bahamas, which played a crucial role in being an important stop in the route of cocaine shipments. Gacha's smuggling logistics, combined with Lehder's knowledge of the latest aerial innovations, paved the way for an ideal partnership, benefitting both equally. Their collaboration was the reason that there was a steady flow of the drug within the U.S. as an expanded outreach of the Cartel's operations.

Contacts With Mexican Cartels

It is interesting to note that Gacha was a Colombian drug smuggler, and he was among the very first drug dealers who established close contacts with the Mexican drug cartels. One of the prominent figures in the Mexican drug trade was Miguel Angel Felix Gallardo, who was the leader of the Guadalajara Cartel. He figured quite rightly that Mexico provided an ideal route to access the U.S. market. Through partnerships with Mexican drug dealers, he built easily accessible, cost-effective, and more secure routes across the U.S.-Mexico border. Through this partnership, he acquired shared profits from the smuggling, a good cache of resources, and the popular nickname "EL Mexico," cementing him as the pioneer of cross-border smuggling.

Alliance With Corrupt Officials and Paramilitary Groups

He also established strong connections with corrupt government officials, military personnel, and law enforcement officials to ensure the secure implementation of operations. He generously used bribery to win over the loyalties of the aforementioned officials and local authorities. His operations were smooth and uninterrupted due to these connections. Also, he actively funded paramilitary forces to guard the routes against attacks by rivals as well as law enforcement. Paramilitary groups also protected Gacha's operations against guerrilla movements like the FARC (Revolutionary Armed Forces of Colombia). These movements were known to mess with the smugglers, especially in the countryside. This protection allowed him to establish his control over the territory of drug routes.

By the end of the 70s, Gonzalo had become one of the most impactful men in Colombia's drug business. Closely associating with Pablo Escobar and many other drug lords elevated his position within the drug trafficking system. Gacha's early life was a story of survival on the tough streets, and he made good use of his intelligence to become one of the kingpins of the drug cartels in Colombia.

CHAPTER 3
EL MEXICANO - THE RISE OF POWER

Gacha's emergence as a drug lord going by the name El Mexicano happened as he expanded his network and influence in cocaine smuggling. He is the pioneer of expanding ties with the Mexican drug lords and exploiting the route to the U.S. through Mexico instead of the Caribbean route. Due to his innovative trafficking techniques, he became a key figure in the Medellin Cartel pretty soon.

Growth and Influence Within the Cartel

When he joined Medellin Cartel, he was a novice just like the enterprise in itself, but he grew into a larger figure of a drug lord enhancing his influence within the cartel. All that happened due to his strategic thinking and violent methods.

Militarization of the Cartel

He played an instrumental role in the expansion of the Medellin Cartel's reach with his aggressive approach and novel techniques. He introduced an organized crime approach to cater to the potential dangers associated with the drug trade. The induction of paramilitary personnel to ensure the safe conduct of smuggling affairs was able to help safeguard the interest of the cartel and fight the rivals in the world of drug smuggling. Gacha incorporated mercenaries and even hitmen to target the potentially dangerous rivals in the drug industry. His idea was that the only way to eliminate the danger was to kill whoever intended to block the proceedings of the trade with no delay or zero compassion for second chances. Interestingly enough, he hired hitmen and paramilitary forces from Mexico, which led to his popular title 'EL MEXICANO." Equally true is the fact that he was the first one to set trends for the militarization of the cartels. He also provided hitmen to the high-profile businessmen in the emerald and drug trade for protection, expanding the influence of the cartel even further.

Gacha's Terror Campaign Against the Colombian Government

His violent methods gave the Colombian government plenty to deal with. He switched his techniques from violence to the use of bribery to win over favors or secure passages to the U.S. for the drug trade, and at other times, the situation demanded an aggressive response to the emergency. His violent methods were not only restricted to mere on-spot shootings or murders; they also encompassed planned assassinations, bombings, and abductions of high-profile figures like journalists, judges, and law enforcement officials. His services came in handy for the cartel to expand its growth, enhance its influence over the world of crime, and help other businessmen. He provided mercenaries for the risk-high figures in trade, thus making him a popular figure and boosting his influence in the competitive world of drug trade.

With the consistent expansion of his network and influence as a drug lord, he accumulated wealth, particularly during the cocaine smuggling and his collaboration with Medellin Cartel. The following are the techniques he applied to expand his influence and growth:

Growth of the Cultivation Area and Refining Capabilities

The most conspicuous feature of his services in the cartel revolved around the plantation of cocaine. He took it upon himself to grow the cocaine plant over vast acres of land he had purchased in the suburbs and out of sight of law enforcement. Thus, he was able to grow cocaine of a high standard at a low cost, increasing the prospects for better profits. This was totally unprecedented as the drug dealers of that time relied on the end product of the drug, cultivated and processed by the unconcerned farmers. Gacha, on the contrary, built a chain of steps before the drug was finally transported for sale. All that, of course, he was able to achieve by first having enough finances to invest in the acres of land for the cocaine cultivation.

Secondly, he built refining plants to process the raw material of the cocaine, transforming it into the final product as a drug for use. This, again, was an unprecedented step into the world of drug trade, cutting his costs and enhancing his profits ultimately. His savings from smuggling the marijuana came in handy as he invested those earnings into building a refining plant to process the cocaine for use.

Gacha's Contribution to Discovering Drug Routes

Other than building his own farms and processing units for the cocaine trade, he also played a significant role in discovering more convenient and safe routes for the transformation of the drugs. He was responsible for creating sophisticated networks for the drug trade, thus ensuring security from rival smugglers as well as from law enforcement personnel. One trademark of his drug trade was that he changed the trend of transporting drugs from the traditional and less secure trade route of the Caribbean to enter the United States by shifting the focus to the Mexican border as an entry into the States.

This not only extended the cartel operations into the Mexican state but also provided a more secure and sophisticated smuggling network. The inclusion of the Mexican territory into the drug trade gave cartels' operations a global reach, starting from Colombia to Mexico, the United States, and eventually to Europe. Building on his connections with the Mexicans, he hired hitmen from the Mexican land to safeguard the routes.

Gacha's Influence Within the Cartel

In little time, he gained a pivotal spot in the operations of the cartel, as his decisions ruled over the decision-making process of the enterprise. He created an influential space for himself among the leadership of the enterprise by suggesting strategic plans, such as paramilitary personnel and tactics for the expansion of the operations.

Besides introducing strategic planning into the operations of cartel, he also collaborated with international drug lords to increase its influence and outreach globally. His alliances with Mexican cartels and international drug tycoons are worth mentioning here. He used these connections for the interests of the cartel: to define safe routes and transportation and distribution spots.

He was smart enough to build connections with government officials as well as law enforcement personnel. In other words, he was able to build relationships with external factors to make the distribution of the drug convenient. He also impacted the internal dynamics of the cartel's operations through strategic decision-making.

Hence, in the later part of the 70s, his position in the cartel underwent a change. His early success in trafficking cocaine helped him to organize an efficient network of suppliers, distributors, and enforcers. From the point of view of the cartel, he was efficient and dangerous due to the violence he brought with him when he was on their team, but against them, he was a dangerous foe. Gacha was able to become the leader of his crew because of his strategic approach and his skills in proper coordination of operations.

Dive Into the International Markets

José Gonzalo Rodríguez Gacha was one of the great masterminds behind expanding Medellin Cartel's operations into the international markets. He enhanced the outreach and influence of cartels in the cocaine trade across the globe through bold initiatives, innovative tactics, and alliances, leading to the domination of Medellin Cartel in the global drug market.

The high-water mark of his career was seen in the early 80s when he gained much control and set up most of his operations. He served a very important function in the Medellín Cartel and was able to play a large part in its activities. He was actively involved in the cartel's control of the global cocaine market, and his connections went much beyond Colombia's territory. The reason Gacha became one of the most significant leaders in the cartel's development was his capacity to add a strategic mind with no mercy. This also made him an important player in the drug business during the period in question.

Expansion of Smuggling Networks

He has always been known for his strategic tactics and creative techniques. Some of his trademarks were creating novel smuggling routes, evading law enforcement, and clashing with rival drug dealers. Before his dominance, the existing drug lord used the traditional routes via air traveling lines and the sea passages; he then came up with much more sophisticated and secure means of transportation, such as semi-submersibles, shipping containers with hidden sections, and light aero transport to commute the cocaine from one part of the globe to another securely. The trade route that the Medellin Cartel followed for cocaine and marijuana smuggling had been restricted to the Caribbean route only, but Gonzalo made the enterprise an international organization with a global outreach spanning Central America, the Caribbean, Europe, and the Gulf of Mexico. The routes proposed and defined under his leadership, became multi-layered networks, making it an uphill task for law enforcement and government officials to chase the drug traders and disrupt their activities.

Novelty in Supply Chain Management

The breakthrough in the supply chain management of the drug trade was marked by the involvement of the front companies in the transportation of the drugs and in laundering money covertly. For that purpose, he approached agricultural companies as well as shipping companies to facilitate the transportation of the drugs and the drug money in the hidden compartments. He also introduced the latest ways of smuggling, which had the technology to evade radar detection. The selection of small submarines, speedboats, and airplanes was a meticulously crafted step for the transferring of drugs across the border because they not only sped up the process but also secured the pathways by evading detection by law enforcement.

Advanced Money Laundering Scheme

Management of the income generated from the drugs is a hell of a task that demands tremendous care to avoid law enforcement and robbers. Gacha's contribution in this regard is also phenomenal as he attempted to devise a proper mechanism and a safe channel for saving as well as transferring the heavy amount of payments securely back to Colombia. Making use of his connections with political officials, front companies, and businessmen, he pioneered the idea of money laundering operations through leading banks such as Panama banks, the Caribbean, the United States, and even shell companies across the borders. The legitimate image of these banks and the companies helped him transport the huge amounts of money safely back to the Caribbean without any security and detection concerns.

He was smart enough to make his black money white through investment in different leading projects of development and infrastructure. For example, he invested huge amounts in booming but also legitimate businesses, such as cattle ranching, hotels, and construction, to make huge sums of black money into white, legitimizing it for general and personal use. These businesses provided cover for his illicit drug trade and helped incorporate his illegitimate money into the mainstream economy.

Taking part in the financial and organizational sides of the cartel work, he became more influential. He was also skilled in managing large cash sums, and the method of washing the money earned by the cartel was essential for its functioning. This enabled him to sink a lot of cash into various ventures while supervising them; they were fronts for money laundering with another corporate cover. In this way, he had considerable influence over the cartel's financial flow as he managed these resources.

Expansion of Medellin Cartel Into Europe

Colombia, being one of the leading growers and transporters of cocaine, eventually realized the demand for the same in Europe. Different countries like Spain, Italy, the Netherlands, and the United Kingdom were the leading customers of Colombian cocaine, with increasing demand for the drug. One wonders how he accessed the European criminal organizations to increase the reach of Medellin Cartel's drug network into the European borders. Utilizing his knack for social skills, he developed strong contacts with the European mafia and smugglers, such as Italian smugglers and the Spanish Galician mafia. These mafia groups were rooted deeply in the black markets of Europe, which were quite effective in the distribution of contraband throughout Europe. Just like Mexican borders are considered ideal for safe transportation, Spain served as an easily accessible and safe entry point for the drug trade into the European continent.

Soon, law enforcement in Europe intensified its control over the borders, causing trouble for the drug smugglers. Even the entry into Europe through Spain became precarious for smuggling, leading to the need to discover new entry points into Europe that are safer to navigate. Gacha could not let go of the bright opportunity to do the drug trade in Europe; with his immaculate skills in logistics of the smuggling routes, he discovered an alternative entry point into Europe for the delivery of cocaine. What alternative route could be more accessible and secure than the West African borders? Since the West African countries are well-known for their weak regional governance, he proposed and actualized the transportation of drugs through this border. Secondly, the West African border was also an ideal option for the drug route for being a strategic location between South America and Europe. Countries like Guinea-Bissau were strategic options for the shipment of cocaine drugs. This proved to be a safer option for bypassing more heavily monitored routes.

Gacha's Hold Into Asian Markets

He confined Medellin Cartel's operations to North America and Europe and expanded them to less established regions. He also pioneered the venture of drug trafficking into the Asian drug market, which was still in its infancy in terms of access to Colombian drugs. Through his social skills, he established strong ties with drug dealers from Japan, Hong Kong, and other parts of Asia. Assessing the growing demand for the drug, he spread his network of shipments to the Asian region, expanding the reach of the cartel even further. His successful reach in the Asian region reflects his ambition to make his drug trade business a global one.

Another important region in which he gained access to drug trafficking was Australia and Oceania due to the increasing demand for cocaine. The affluent class of the region was the ideal consumer of the product, allowing for the country's need for drug supplies. Gacha, through his personal ties with mafia and drug dealers, supplied the cartel's supplies of the drug to the few affluent who proved to be permanent customers. Although the drug markets were still quite small, they yielded profits in high amounts due to the lack of availability of drugs in the region. In other words, high demand but limited supply of the drugs led to an increase in the prices of the drugs.

Top-Down Integration and Hold on Supply Chain

His influence over the Medellin Cartel's drug operations was not only horizontal (shipment of the drug throughout the globe ranging from North America, Europe, Asia, Australia, and Oceania) but also vertical(top-down integration of the drug). Gacha was instrumental in managing the vertical integration of the cartel's operations by growing large swaths of coca in Colombian areas such as Magdalena

Valley and the eastern plains under his close observation. Besides the production, he also supervised the refining and processing of the drug, which helped him directly control the supply of the drug, reducing reliance on the third party. It also made the cocaine supply pure, abundant, and cost-effective. With the passage of time, cocaine supplied by the Medellin Cartel emerged as an international brand, attracting demand from across the globe for its purity and high quality, amassing profits for the Medellin Cartel as well as for himself.

Gonzalo Gacha's Influence on His International Ventures

His international ventures expanded the market of Colombian cocaine throughout the globe and naturally added to the revenues of the Medellin Cartel. From being a novice and just a loosely operated enterprise, the Medellin Cartel emerged as one of the most influential cartels that increased demand for cocaine as far as Australia and Oceania. The more revenue it generated, the more finances it had to invest in further expansion and solidification of the trafficking network. He became a single source of drug supplies in North America, Europe, the Asian Region, and Australia, rendering it indispensable for supplies.

Assessing the stronghold and the expansion of Medellin Cartel under the leadership of Jose Rodriguez Gonzalo Gacha as a drug lord, law enforcement tightened its hold on the trade to control drug smuggling. Before the emergence of the Medellin Cartel, drug smuggling was considered a less serious crime. However, the way it expanded its networks across the globe in such a short time put the government and law enforcement on guard to not only put a check on their activities but also to declare it as a serious crime. As a result, law enforcement agencies formulated a coordinated response to deal with the threatening situation of the drug mafia for the very first time. One such example to quote here is that of the U.S. DEA, which intensified its efforts to locate and destroy the expanding networks of the Medellin Cartel worldwide, putting a lot of pressure on the workings of the cartel.

As mentioned earlier, Gacha was known for his ruthlessness and aggression; he also pioneered the use of paramilitary forces in the world of the mafia for smooth functioning as well as for protection. Due to his violent methods, he was also approached by tycoons in the business and mafia world to provide bodyguards. His collaboration with other criminal organizations, such as Mexican drug lords and the European mafia, bolstered the stronghold of the Medellin Cartel and also made the drug trade an organized crime. Some direct outcomes of these alliances with global criminal organizations were the diversification of smuggling routes, establishment of new markets, and innovation of methods for the conduction of illicit trade.

Hence, geographic and operational diversification was another major influence that propelled him toward the top. He adeptly sealed cocaine conduits in various sections, particularly the vital trafficking channels in Columbia and other adjacent countries. Since he dominated these routes, he was in a position to influence some terms between himself and the suppliers and distributors, hence enhancing his position in the cartel. His business expanded to America, where he effectively contributed to the supply of cocaine to many cities, making him a crucial member of the cartel.

The Mexican Connection

Gacha's popular title, "El Mexicano," speaks volumes about his connections with the Mexican drug mafia. The Mexican connection played a great role in transforming the drug trade and the position of Medellin Cartel vis-a-vis the world of organized crime and drug mafia. Following are the ways in which he benefited from the Mexican connections:

Strategic Collaborations

Building on his networks and connections with like-minded people, he established strategic ties with the Mexican drug lords. Realizing that the Mexican border as a far better and more secure entry point into the United States than the previous one through the Caribbean coast, he started forming alliances with the drug lords of the region. He had a strong collaboration with the leading Mexican drug cartel named Guadalajara. At that time, the cartel was being led by Miguel Angel Felix Gallardo, who was one of the most powerful drug lords in the 1980s. It was his insight and foresight that made him discover the primary gateway for Colombian cocaine into the United States.

Reciprocal Benefiting Situation

Benefitted a lot from his connections with the great Mexican drug lord Miguel Angel Felix Gallardo and the newly discovered Mexican border entry point into the United States, but this alliance was not merely one-sided. The collaboration was mutually advantageous as Gacha proved quite beneficial to the Mexican cartels for providing adequate supplies of pure quality, homegrown cocaine to the Mexican cartels and drug factions. They were provided with high-quality cocaine to Mexican groups as payment for offering the Mexican workforce to transport cocaine across the United States-

Mexico border. They distributed the drugs in Mexico as well as the United States.

Deployment of Mexican Contract Fighters

Keeping in mind the security concerns associated with the drug business, as well as the need to establish the hegemony of the Medellin Cartel over important territories and the smuggling routes, he came up with the solution of hiring paramilitary forces. They had multifarious roles (ranging from hitmen to bodyguards) to secure the trafficking routes. For that purpose, he hired paramilitary forces from Mexico as mercenaries; it was his affinity with the Mexicana which earned him the title "El Mexico." These mercenaries were usually chosen as people who were former soldiers or trained bodyguards or killers with already learned skills for fighting and military tactics. This incorporation of paramilitary forces rendered Medellin Cartel the flavor of brutality and violence but nevertheless improved the cartel's effectiveness.

Gacha played quite an instrumental role in the funding and training of the paramilitary groups. There was also the conspicuous participation of Mexican nationals be it in terms of training, funding, and being part of the force. This force was trained and formed to provide protection against rivals, secure the operation routes, and combat Colombian guerillas who were deployed to threaten the interests of cartels.

Violence became a characteristic of the cartel, and Gacha himself was one of the participants in the horrible crimes committed by the organization. His inclination towards the use of force to enforce authority, including in matters of conflict, made him a rather rough character. Such a reputation was valuable not only for gaining an advantage over potential competitors but also for inducing obedience among the employees. Through control over the private army of enforcers, he was able to use a fair extent of coercion and intimidation, which was particularly important for building and maintaining power within the cartel.

Spread of Smuggling Networks

His collaboration with the Mexican drug lords also resulted in the diversification of the smuggling routes, ranging from air to land to underwater, dodging law enforcement agencies. These routes crossed over land and maritime passages for drug trafficking via the Pacific Ocean and the Gulf of Mexico. Small airplanes were utilized through the air routes to transport the drugs globally. The most conspicuous feature of these transportation means was that they were quite diverse as well as efficient in escaping radar detection by law enforcement.

The Mexican collaboration also helped him develop innovative, creative, and sophisticated methods for drug trafficking. These methods included hiding the drug supplies or the earned money in the hidden compartments of the vehicles. Gacha was overambitious about building a safe and secure route across the United States-Mexico border, as he went to the extent of building underground tunnels to commute the drugs safely without being detected by law enforcement. Moreover, for under-the-water commute, he built semi-submarines and speedboats for cocaine trafficking. This diversity in the drug trafficking routes helped a lot in the secure smuggling of drugs throughout the globe.

Building Drug Sanctuaries in Mexico

The building of sanctuaries or safe havens for drug operations was made possible due to collaboration with Mexico. That was because Mexico could offer a logistic base for Medellin Cartel's drug operations. Taking advantage of the geographical and strategic location of Mexico, Gacha constructed safety houses, warehouses, and front companies for various purposes, including storing and trafficking the drug, converting the black money of smuggling into white money by investing in front companies, and finally coordinating logistics. These drug sanctuaries and safe havens provided the location for the shipment of drugs from Colombia into Mexico and finally to the United States and farther away.

In alliance with the Mexican drug lords and mafia, he tried to win over law enforcement with bribery in order to make drug trafficking even more risk-free. He offered bribery in adequate amounts to win over local officials, law enforcement, and border agents for smooth operation and commute of the drugs across the border, minimizing the interdiction. By this point, he had characterized himself as quite ruthless and violent, so much so that he wasted no time eliminating the potential danger. In addition, his collaboration with the Mexican lords made him learn the worth of bribing the concerned government officials and law enforcement to secure the drug smuggling operations through key transit points.

Personal Affinity With the Mexicans

Gacha had a personal affinity with the Mexican culture, which made him embrace the Mexican persona. His fascination for the Mexican culture is reflected through his adoption of its cowboy and charro traditions. It was not a surprise to see him attired in a cowboy style with a hat and long boots in the style of cowboys. He also loved listening to Mariachi music, which is the traditional music of Mexico. His love for Mexico did not end with wearing cowboy-style clothes and enjoying Mariachi music; he went to the extent of owning ranches in Mexico. His love for the Mexican culture and identity brought him closer to the Mexican cartels and helped him secure favors from the drug lords when he was still new to the world of organized crime.

He built close connections with the drug lords of Mexico not only to the extent of professional needs only. According to some reports, he developed personal relations with mainstream Mexican families who were quite active in drug trafficking. These personal ties with families helped him strengthen his influence in Mexico. After just a little time, he was quite rooted in the Mexican drug smuggling landscape only due to his adoption of Mexican culture and identity.

Influence of Ties With Mexico

Gacha's ties with the Mexican drug lords had several effects on his emergence as a drug lord as well as on the dynamics of the Mexican drug market. First of all, it made the position and the drug trafficking operations of the Medellin Cartel stronger. The Medellin Cartel picked up the pace in strengthening its hold on the drug trafficking market through its alliance with Mexican drug lords to access Mexican smuggling routes. The access to the routes helped the enterprise enhance its cocaine trafficking operations. These Mexican borders provided unprecedented safe, secure, and efficient routes to transport drugs into the United States.

Provided a Base for the Rise of Gacha as a Billionaire Drug Lord

The groundwork for the future rise of the Mexican cartels in the world of organized crime was laid down by this Mexican-Medellin Cartel partnership. The rising Mexican drug dealers learned a huge deal from Gacha's drug smuggling logistics, diversification of the transport system, and accumulation of paramilitary forces. On top of that, to repay Mexican drug dealers for offering their border as an entry point into the United States, he provided a steady supply of cocaine drug to the Mexican drug lords. The supplies of high-quality cocaine helped them stretch their dominance and influence over the drug market, which led to their eventual rise as leading players in the drug market across the globe.

Heightened U.S. Law Enforcement Attention

On the one hand, the increased and organized activities of drug trafficking led to strengthened Medellin Cartel and Mexican cartels' activities, but on the other hand, it put law enforcement and government officials on guard to check these drug smuggling activities. The diversified routes and the complex methods for transporting drugs across the globe made it challenging for law enforcement and government agencies to destroy the stronghold of the cartels' activities. Mexico-Gacha ties stand as a testament to foresight and potential as a future billionaire drug lord who merely originated from a humble background. It played an instrumental role in increasing the Medellin Cartel's reach and influence for generations to come.

Becoming an International Name

One of the reasons Jose Rodriguez Gonzalo Gacha became an international name in the world of organized crime was because of his active involvement in the global drug smuggling market. His collaboration with the Mexican cartels and discovery of the Mexican border as an entry point for supplying cocaine to the United States to supply cocaine and set new trends in the drug mafia. As a prize for providing the border for transportation, he provided steady supplies of high-quality cocaine to Mexican drug lords, spreading the drug use and smuggling even further. He increased Medellin Cartel's reach beyond Mexican borders to the Asian region, Europe, and then later on to Australia, the United States considered drug trafficking as a heinous crime worth a serious penalty. Hunting down the international figure like him became the primary goal of law enforcement agencies, which culminated in his death at the hands of such personnel. At the peak of his career and notoriety, his name became synonymous with the global drug trade. He became a prominent figure, a billionaire drug lord figure in the history of the organized crime of drug smuggling.

Over the span of a few decades, he spread the network of diverse transportation routes, safe havens for cultivating, processing, and storing cocaine till ready for transportation across the globe, earning him the status of an international criminal figure. This international reach became one of the primary reasons for him gaining notoriety worldwide.

Hence, as is evident from his title "EL MEXICANO," his collaboration with the Mexican drug lords and cartels played a significant role in extending the reach of the Medellin Cartel in the global drug market. This era is marked by the rise to power of Gacha, Medellin Cartel, and the Mexican drug lords across the globe.

CHAPTER 4
THE FOES - LAW ENFORCEMENT, RIVALS, AND INTERNAL CONFLICTS

Jose Rodriguez Gonzalo Gacha was one of the most feared and aggressive drug lords of the cartel. After he secured his success, notoriety, and international reach, it was natural to have an army of rivals and internal conflicts, as well as a fixed threat from law enforcement agencies. El Mexicano's climb up his organization's ranks led him to become involved in conflict with a wide range of opponents. His criminal empire was based on the sale of cocaine and the organization of violence. Its consequences fostered a large number of opponents from within the criminal world as well as from the police departments. His enemies and rivals played a vital role in defining his criminal activity and commitment. In addition, they greatly influenced the precariousness and deadly nature of drug trafficking in Colombia in the 1980s.

Gacha Vs. Law Enforcement

As a result of his fast-paced rise as a drug lord and the expansion of the Medellin Cartel's network, he had extensive conflicts with law enforcement in Colombia and the United States. To cater to the situation, he employed various techniques depending on the requirements of the situation. For example, the situation would sometimes demand a violent confrontation with law enforcement agencies; at other times, it called for strategic bribery and manipulation.

Bribery, Trickery, and Manipulation

When he was still in the early stage of his career as a drug lord and he had not developed relationships with the drug lords and the concerned cartels, he resorted to trickery to manipulate law enforcement. For that purpose, he gave bribes to the local police and military officials to make his drug operations smooth without the threat of capture or disruption. He needed the support of law enforcement not only for drug transportation but also to protect his coca plantation farms and processing plants to evade disruptions from the police and the military. In areas like his hometown of Pacho in Cundinamarca, there was a dominance of politicians. To protect his illegal activities, he had to offer incentives and bribes to the politicians instead of police and military officials. The other areas were where he had installed refining plants to process the cocaine for final use. He needed to be protected from raid, and he needed to avoid being captured. In order to protect the plains of Meta and the jungles of Caqueta, he used bribery and incentives to influence the police, military, and politicians.

He also initiated the expansion of his network and the relationships with corrupt law enforcement officials by investing heavily in them. His trick of financially benefitting the corrupt officials worked wonderfully to keep his activities related to cocaine plantation, processing of the drug, and drug smuggling unchecked for many years to come. This particularly came in handy during the period when he was still quite new to the drug business and had little contact with the leading drug lords of the time.

His trickery in dealing with law enforcement was not restricted to merely financial gains; he proved himself quite helpful in terms of providing intelligence to law enforcement about the activities of the rival drug traffickers. The ratting out of the rival drug lords and their activities helped him in various ways, including evading the disruptions from law enforcement in return for eliminating the potential competition from the rival drug cartels.

Combating Law Enforcement Through Aggression

His second and more popular strategy of dealing with law enforcement was violence and the induction of paramilitary forces. His aggression, ruthlessness, and knack for violence gained him quite a reputation with the leading drug cartels in Colombia as well as in Mexico.

Gacha also adopted an aggressive approach against the attacks from law enforcement. Late in his career, he acquired quite a reputation as a leading drug lord in the world of organized crime; he resorted more to violence as a core strategy to deal with law enforcement and protection of drug smuggling. As part of his strategy, he was responsible for the assassinations of various high-profile people like police officers, judges, prosecutors, government officials, and whoever was adamant in wiping out the drug smuggling-related activities.

One manifestation of his violent activities includes the bomb explosion in 1989. In order to protect his self-interests, he planned and executed the bombings of the headquarters of the Department of Administrative Security (DAS) in Bogota, which resulted in the killings of dozens of people (United Nations Office on Drugs and Crime, 2017). His intention was merely to spread terror for the

Medellin Cartel. And it was one of many orchestrated attacks targeting government institutions and law enforcement agencies.

He did not restrict his violent activities to the bombings of the buildings alone; he also orchestrated the formation of death squads. The job of these squads was to attack law enforcement personnel in order to prevent them from disrupting the drug activities of Medellin Cartel. To achieve the smooth functioning of the Medellin Cartel, Gacha trained these death squads for the assassinations, kidnappings, and bombings to steer clear of the hurdles. He was known for his fearlessness and ruthlessness to kill the problem-causing officials and personnel on the spot without even giving it a second thought. This strategy helped him create an intimidating image of his enterprise, Medellin Cartel, among the rival factions as well as law enforcement agencies.

Targeting the Police and Military Office

Gacha did not shy away from taking bold steps when it raised a question regarding self-protection and the protection of drug activities. One of the greatest hurdles in the way of his illegal activities was the one posed by the police and the military personnel. With the rise of the drug trade, which was initiated in his era due to his innovative logistics in the drug trade, law enforcement agencies and government officials suddenly became active as far as combating his activities. Hence, they were one of the leading threats and disruptions to his life and business activities. But his aggression and ruthlessness did not spare anyone, including the police and the military. In the late 1980s, when Gacha had strengthened his position as a drug lord with the network of his illegal drug trade that had spread all across the globe, he deployed special task forces whose job was to execute direct assaults on the police and military bases. He deployed his forces in sensitive areas like transportation routes, cocaine farms, and refining plants for protection against law enforcement disruptions. He had a reputation for going beyond all the limits and waging a direct war against state forces threatening his drug activities. His combat strategies were also quite untraditional and callous.

For example, on one occasion, he executed an attack on a police station in El Dorado, Meta. He had cocaine plantation farms and refining labs in Meta, but perceiving that they could be under attack, the cartel members—in alliance with local mercenaries—assaulted the police station, which resulted in the killings of multiple police officers. He also used paramilitary forces to protect his assets from law enforcement.

Deployment of Paramilitary Personnel and Alliances

He was a trendsetter in terms of deploying paramilitary forces and forming alliances with right-wing paramilitary groups in Colombia and later on in Mexico. These militias helped him protect his cocaine plantation farms, refining units, and smuggling routes against attack from law enforcement agencies. Proving that nothing comes without a cost, Gacha paid heavily to take care of the funding as well as providing arms to several forces.

Making use of these paramilitary forces, he also created semi-military forces who were trained to engage directly with the law enforcement forces of Colombia for the protection of cocaine smuggling routes. Through the formation of these alliances, he helped the Medellin Cartel maintain control over the important territories and the traffic routes throughout the state. He strategically planned the spread of drug traffic routes to pass through the villages, small towns, and countryside where the hold of law enforcement was quite weak.

Escalation of Conflict With the Rise of Gacha as a Drug Lord

The rise of billionaire drug lord happened somewhere after the mid-1980s; the time coincided with the expansion of the Medellin Cartel's network across the globe for drug smuggling. It was during this time that law enforcement and the government of Colombia, as well as the United States, categorized drug trafficking as a serious crime that needed to be checked with immediate effect. Declaring the activities of Jose Rodriguez Gonzalo Gacha and the Medellin Cartel as illegal, the United States and Colombian government initiated their war against the drug mafia to target the potential dangers in the mid-1980s. Due to the escalation of the drug trade and violent activities by Medellin Cartel, he was announced as the most wanted public enemy in Colombia and the United States.

Gacha, owing to his aggressive nature, did not stop short of declaring an open war against the law enforcement personnel and the government institutes. The infamous 1989 bombings of the headquarters of the Department of Administrative Security (DAS) in Bogota and the attack on police and military bases are a few examples of counterattacks managed by Gacha and Medellin Cartel to spread terror in the states (Long, 1989). In order to protect himself, his drug activities, and the functioning of the cartels, he financed as well as launched various violent attacks, including targeted killings and public assassinations of judges and politicians.

Keeping in view the escalated drug crimes and the violent attacks on law enforcement, the United States signed an extradition treaty with the Colombian government for the arrest or dismantling of Gacha or Medellin Cartel's drug activities. He specifically targeted those personnel and the politicians who favored the extradition treaty with the United States. The violent attacks by his paramilitary forces were defensive and vindictive but also were planned to spread a feeling of intimidation, fear, and chaos, dissuading the authorities from chasing him and his drug activities.

Impact on Law Enforcement Strategies

As the saying goes, violence begets violence. The increased militarization of approach to combat cartels (particularly the Medellin Cartel and its drug activities) led to a more violent response. In response to this, law enforcement agencies formed collaborations with various law force factions to effectively dismantle Medellin Cartel, and their activities. They formed alliances with United States agencies like the DEA, CIA, and FBI to ensure the capture of the invincible and formidable Gacha and the drug cartel. These alliances, amid different law agencies and police bases, served to share intelligence, impart training, and conduct joint operations.

The other purpose of the collaboration of law enforcement was to conduct anti-narcotics campaigns to make the country drug-free. They conducted intelligence-led operations against drug cartels and key figures like, who were quite active in the drug smuggling business. They especially targeted the drug dealers in the leadership ladder of the cartels to make their combat strategies more effective and efficient. For that purpose, they deployed informants who were assigned the task of researching the secret operation routes and the related intelligence for dismantling drug operations. They also deployed task forces and specialized units to counteract the paramilitary violent activities that had been developed by drug lords.

Gacha's violent activities, like bombings of government institutes and paramilitary attacks on police and military bases, led to public opinion against him, the Medellin Cartel, and their drug activities. They endorsed the aggressive efforts of law enforcement and government actions against them, leading to changes in the legislation and legal rules. For the first time, the governments of Colombia and the United States passed anti-drug laws and policies that were aimed at extradition to the United States. This was a hallmark as it allowed the transfer of such criminals and drug dealers to the United States for persecution within U.S. courts.

The Colombian government and its agencies that used police and military force also proved to be a strong and determined opponent. Colombia was at the time waging war on drug barons, and Gacha was a prime target of government forces. Drugs were strictly prohibited, and the government did not spare any effort to fight drug traffickers. Since he was a major player in criminal activities, he emerged on the radar of the police and other law agencies.

Jose Gacha and His Rivals

He gained unprecedented popularity, maximizing his network across the globe in the world of organized crime in just a little time. His association with the existing drug lords like Pablo Escobar and the Medellin Cartel also made him a billionaire drug lord, which many drug dealers could only aspire to achieve. His aggressive methods to kill the hurdles, be it law enforcement personnel or a rival faction on the spot, combined with competitive and strategic logistics skills, made him a potential threat to the rival drug lords and the cartels. It was natural for him to be surrounded by rival factions who wanted to eliminate his name just to take his clientele and dominance in the world of crime and drug smuggling. Following are the rival groups which were constantly in conflict with Gacha:

The Cali Cartel

Another serious competitor was the Cali Cartel, which was headed by the Rodríguez Orejuela brothers, Gilberto and Miguel. The Cali Cartel was rivals with the Medellín Cartel, and the two Bogotá groups were mainly involved in conflict over territorial and control of cocaine. The conflict between the two cartels was sharp and cruel; Medellín and Cali cartels tried to eliminate each other's influence in the country as much as they could. Since Gacha was one of the most important members of the Medellín Cartel, he was an active participant in this ongoing war, and the Cali Cartel rivaled the Medellín cartel in narcotics trafficking.

The Cali Cartel was one of the earliest rivals of the Medellin Cartel. They were known for their business-oriented approach to conducting drug trafficking, but they were extremely competitive and gave quite a tough competition to the Medellin Cartel. His aggressive methods resulted in violent clashes and assassinations of each other's cartel members.

Fabio Ochoa Vásquez

Another rival drug lord who posed quite a tough competition to him was Fabio Ochoa Vasquez. He was also one of the prominent members of the Medellin Cartel, and it was presumed that he was friends with Gonzalo. But the reality was a bit different as they did not get along with each other, resulting in frequent tussles. They had a different set of ideologies in terms of approaches to the drug trade system. The differences in the approaches included business outlook, the distribution of profits, and the ways to handle law enforcement pressure. The main difference between the two leading drug lords was due to the method of conducting the drug business. Just like Cali Cartel, Fabio Ochoa Vasquez also had a business-oriented approach to drug smuggling in contrast to Gacha's aggressive methods of bombing, assassinations, explosions, and target killings.

Carlos Lehder

One more important name in the list of rivals was Carlos Lehder. Carlos played an important role in the transportation of cocaine to the United States. For smooth transportation reasons, he traveled on his personal airstrip on Norman's Cay in the Bahamas. He was quite an important member of the Medellin Cartel, who played an instrumental role in ensuring the smooth trafficking of drugs. He had a very different personality in comparison to Cali and Fabio, with an aura of flamboyancy and a touch of Nazi ideology reflected in his dealings. Even though Jose Gacha had a similar personality with a preference for aggression and violence, both of them did not get along. These clashes in the methodology led to conflicts, creating fissures within the enterprise of the Medellin Cartel.

Jorge Luis Ochoa Vásquez

Jorge Luis Ochoa Vasquez was also one of the leading members of the Medellin Cartel, but Gacha was not able to get along with him either. Just like Fabio, Ochoa had some essential differences in strategy for drug smuggling, which became one of the leading causes of the conflicts between them. Other than that, the territorial control for drug smuggling and distribution was the key point for clashes. Also, financial matters caused rifts between the two countries. These differences among different members of Medellin Cartel, became a prime reason for the internal rifts and conflict in the enterprise. The other members collectively had issues with the aggressive and violent techniques of Gacha for drug trafficking. They also didn't think too highly of the spread of terror caused by his unique approach.

Griselda Blanco

Blanco, popularly known by names the "Black Widow" or " La Madrina," was also one of the instrumental players of the Medellin Cartel. She was an active member of the early operations of the cartel. She was especially active during the 1970s and early 1980s in the Miami region because of her aggressive methods. Blanco was an extremely brutal and callous leader who got things done the way she wanted. Her violent temperament became one of the prime reasons for falling out with the other members of the Medellin Cartel. Her aggressive methods and ambition to establish control over her empire became a valid cause for conflicts with other members of the cartel, especially Gacha. Her overambition eventually led to her exile from the enterprise's power structures.

Rafael Caro Quintero

Rafael Caro Quintero was also not a member of the Medellin Cartel, but he had a rivalry with Gacha, which culminated in violent attacks. Quintero was the co-founder of the Guadalajara Cartel in Mexico. It is true that Rafael was not a direct rival to him; in other words, he never directly fell out with him ever, but his stronghold on the drug trade provided him with the power base that could put any other drug lord into the situation of rivalry and envy, leading to complex relationships with Colombian drug lords. For example, the Medellin Cartel and Guadalajara Cartel always had daggers drawn at each other over routes, markets, and alliances. Moreover, Gacha's undue affinity with the Mexican culture became a constant source of conflicts over the division of territories or profits.

Amado Carrillo Fuentes ("El Señor de los Cielos")

Amado Carrillo Fuentes was also one of the key players in the cocaine trade. He was the leader of the Juarez Cartel in Mexico and was popular because of being an indispensable member who transported the cocaine drugs through aircraft, posing direct competition to Gacha's unique method of transportation. Despite being partners in business relations, they had conflicts over lucrative routes, profits, and drug markets, leading to clashes and rivalry between the two cartels.

Hélmer "Pacho" Herrera

Being a leading figure in the Cali Cartel, Helmer "Pacho" Herrera emerged as a prominent rival to the Medellin Cartel. One of the prime reasons for rivalry was his position in terms of power structure in the world of organized crime; to be specific, he had widespread control over large portions of the cocaine trade. Due to his control, he established his kind of monopoly over the United States East Coast markets. Posing direct competition to the dealings of the Medellin Cartel in drug operations became a big cause of frequent conflicts and confrontations.

Victor Carranza ("The Emerald King")

Victor Carranza, also known as "The Emerald King," had been one of the most instrumental figures in the emerald trade. He had also served as a paramilitary leader in the Colombian drug trade business. Due to his vested interests in the emerald trade financially, he had conflicts with the functioning of the Medellin Cartel, particularly with Gacha. They clashed over control of the Boyaca, the region that is popularly known as a rich source of emerald mines. Because of financial issues, they engaged in violent clashes, resulting in the killing of members from both factions. Their common goal was to establish sole control over the territory and its reservoirs of emerald.

The aggressive and violent methods of Jose Rodriguez Gonzalo Gacha became one of the primary reasons for direct clashes and confrontations with drug lords outside the Medellin Cartel. His increasing control and expanding kingdom of drug smuggling made him a rival to the leading drug lords. The rivalries had different flavors ranging from alliances, betrayals, and outright warfare, leading to the overall image of Colombia as a bloody and complex place to live in, particularly during the 1980s.

Inevitably, Gacha faced threats from multiple criminal groups as well as other constituencies within the criminal fraternity. Set in a time of more organized warfare, his world was filled with betrayal and ambiguous enemies, in which he had to switch between the two sides and make cold, calculated moves in defense of his clan's rights.

It would not be an exaggeration to assert that José Rodríguez Gacha had an impressive list of enemies and rivals as a result of his criminal activities, in particular representatives of the Cali Cartel and the Colombian police. There was plenty of conflict, and he had to maneuver his way to the top in the futile war of the drug cartels as well as the standoff against the government. These adversaries contributed to his development and either directly or indirectly enhanced violence in the drug business during the period.

Gacha Vs. His Own People

Gacha, due to his unprecedented fame, violence, and strategic outlook, faced not only external conflicts but also internal conflicts. Other drug lords from within the Medellin Cartel posed as rivals to him over methods of drug smuggling, ideology of the business, and competition. It was his ruthlessness, terror, and paranoia that led to significant tensions among the cartel members.

Multiple groups within the cartel, as well as insolent subordinates, could and did challenge his supremacy. Civil war of this sort was a persistent problem, and to keep things running without constant upheaval, he had to maintain balance within his organization.

Rivalries From Within

He had a unique relationship with the leading drug lord of the Medellin Cartel, Pablo Escobar, who was also his initial ally in the drug trade. As Gacha rose through the ranks, the alliance turned into a rivalry. Pablo did not actually like his free and independent style because he thought his intent was merely self-enhancement regardless of the overall growth of the cartel. He also didn't like his inclination for violent methods and his diverse goals. Pablo wanted the cartel to focus on the cocaine trade only, but Gacha wanted to include other important trades, including marijuana and emeralds, into the endeavors of the cartel administration. The conflict grew as he felt threatened due to a direct challenge to his leadership role in the Medellin Cartel.

His other internal rivals included the Ochoa brothers (Fabio, Jorge Luis, and Juan David), who clashed with him because their diplomatic business-oriented style was at odds with his violent approach. Besides the Ochoa brothers, Victor Carranza also posed a threat to Gacha because of competition over the Colombian emerald trade and the rich sources of emerald mining in the regions of Boyaca.

Internal Purges and Paranoia

Gacha had open conflicts with some members of the Medellin Cartel, and it was natural for him to feel general paranoia and threats from within the enterprise. As a result, he started looking at members from within his enterprise as potential enemies who were looking for opportunities to rat him out as soon as the opportunity struck. He castigated his members for being informants or the ones actively plotting against him. In order to cater to his paranoia and purify the cartel, he conducted several purges, killing anyone who had the remotest link with the betrayal or the potential for being a traitor. This led to an overall distrustful and intimidating atmosphere within the organization. As a part of the purge campaign, he even shot his loyal members on the slightest clues and suspicions, causing cartel members to distrust Gacha himself. Even loyal members were convinced to started aligning with his rivals within the cartel. The atmosphere of fear and district hardly brought about any good; rather, it led to a weakening of the faction, as his members preferred to distance themselves from him.

Rivalry with His Blood Relations, Including His Son

Fredy Rodriguez Celades, the son of Jose Rodriguez Gonzalo Gacha, was also not spared from his father's paranoia. There were always clashes regarding certain drug operations, even though his son was actively involved in the operations. He also had some issues regarding the strategic logistics of the drug trade. His son thought more pragmatically and disapproved of his father's violent methods, which became a primary source of disagreements.

Other than violent methods, his knack for unilateral decision-making techniques also led to various conflicts and issues with those close to him. His close associates thought that his aggressive moves like bombings, assassinations, and attacks on police and military bases put law enforcement on guard against the drug trade, creating more problems for the cartel rather than intimidating the government and law enforcement agencies. Close associates, including his bodyguards, did not feel secure due to his suspicion of them. This affected their loyalty to him.

Clashes Over the Use of Financial Resources

There was friction among some members of the Medellin Cartel regarding the usage of financial resources. These members thought that he was quite generous and rather casual about the spending of these resources. He did not hesitate to invest the money earned from his personal endeavors; these investments included acquiring new lands for plantation or other purposes or even hiring paramilitary forces to use his aggressive methods. His spending decisions were a significant point of discord for other members who wanted to spend the amount to expand the cartel's operations. Of course, there were individuals who wanted those funds equally distributed among all members of the cartel, especially the partners.

There were also conflicts over how to handle law enforcement agencies, who worked extra hard to try and shut down the operations of the Medellin Cartel. The only solutions lay in instigating violence and creating an atmosphere of fear through bombs and attacks. Others within his orbit wanted more pragmatic coping strategies, leading to more complex issues between Gacha and other members.

Impact of Internal Rivalries

One significant impact of internal conflicts and rivalries was the ultimate downfall, because the conflicts led to a lack of trust and mutual respect among the members, particularly the partners and the leaders. Gacha's extreme violence, paired with his paranoia, disrupted the unity of the cartel, leading to a gradual disfigurement of the organization as a whole. Gradually, he became distant and isolated from the other members of the cartel, leading to the weakening of ties among the partners of the cartel. The decline of the Medellin Cartel came as good news for law enforcement agencies, as it became easier to hunt down Gacha specifically. The one who used to rat out rival drug lords for his self-interests became the one being ratted out, as rival members provided intelligence to law enforcement personnel.

Secondly, the atmosphere of paranoia and fear had a trickle-down effect, as it led the rise of betrayal and disloyalty. Fearing that they might be hunted down by Gacha due to his personal paranoia over disloyalty, some men ratted him out to the authorities, resulting in fateful 1989 encounter.

The paranoia and the internal conflict led to an overall decrease in the cohesion of the Medellin Cartel. Even the loyal members felt exasperated due to the bickering and tussles within the cartel. All the internal conflict made it easier for law enforcement authorities who were determined to hunt him down.

To sum it up, his overambition, competitiveness, and paranoia led to the emergence of conflicts and rivals from within as well as outside the Medellin Cartel. It was because of internal conflicts that he was finally hunted down by law enforcement authorities years later.

CHAPTER 5
THE END OF AN ERA - THE DOWNFALL OF DON SOMBRERO

Gacha's association with the Medellín Cartel and the Colombian production and exportation of cocaine did establish him as a power dealer in the criminal fraternity, but the events that led to his death could be described as a roller coaster. That was during the early 1980s, when he had firmly cemented his place in the Medellín Cartel. His administrative and managerial style was marked by strategic decision-making, and his lack of scruples helped him to increase the cartel's power in both domestic and foreign spheres.

However, this period also saw the group in dominance for a while, but it faced serious battles with other rival cartels and pressure from the Colombian government. The Cali Cartel, led by the Rodríguez Orejuela brothers, was one of the main rivals of Gacha. The struggle for control of the drug corridors and the distribution channels turned into a confrontation between the two most significant cartels, Medellín and Cali. These confrontations also escalated the violence and also brought crucial attention from police and other governmental organs. His doom was a result of these conflicts, especially because of the violence and instability these conflicts brought into the region.

The First Crack in His Power

The first crack in the supremacy of Jose Gonzalo Rodriguez Gacha had a trickle-down effect, leading to further fissures, ushering in the end of an era. That first crack happened in 1988 when his ventures failed one after another due to strategic errors of the Medellin Cartel that put law enforcement on guard. The efforts of cartel members to undermine the intelligence of Gacha within the cartel and other narcotic networks—just out of envy and jealousy—put not only him but also the Medellin Cartel at stake. Following is the list of key events that led to his eventual downfall, ending an era of drug smuggling for particularly Medellin Cartel:

- ❖ His first mishap was an assault on the U.S. Embassy in 1988 as he made a huge mistake in the analysis of the situation, leading to his eventual downfall. Just to build pressure and terrorize the law enforcement agencies, he planned and executed an attack on the United States Embassy in Bogota. The plan to bomb the building using a car bomb failed; this resulted in an intense reaction on the part of the United States, which collaborated with the Colombian Government to capture him and stop the drug trade activities of his cartel. The collaboration of the United States in the capture of Gacha and the members of the Medellin Cartel reflects the seriousness and commitment of the rivals internationally to bring down his downfall.

- ❖ The second error of judgment on the part of Jose Gacha was his involvement in the slaughter of the local people of Kankuamo in late 1987. This was carried out on the mere assumption that these people were responsible for ratting out secret information about the whereabouts and the drug trade logistics as well as the networks of the Cartel Medellin. Upon the slightest clue that they were involved in providing the secret information about the marijuana operations of Medellin Cartel, he ordered the massacre of 19 Kankuamo local people belonging to the Sierra Nevada de Santa Marta region. It was an error of judgment as it proved false later on; however, it triggered widespread protests in Colombia demanding action against the outrage from both Colombian and international law enforcement agencies. His ruthlessness led to more resentment from the common public and built pressure to track him down and end the brutalities.

❖ There were also instances of betrayal and intelligence leaks, particularly from within his organizations. For example, it was quite shocking to discover that his former friend and confidant did not shy away from ratting out the secrets about his drug operations and illegal activities to the law enforcement agencies from both the Colombian government as well as the United States. It was Evaristo Porras who leaked intelligence, providing law enforcement insight into his networks and their logistics, leading to the initial erosion of his dominance and disruption of his drug operations.

Jose Gacha not only handled the drug trade, transporting the drugs across the globe but also taking it upon himself to oversee the cultivation and processing of drugs, including cocaine and marijuana. The vast spans of marijuana and cocaine plantation and the refining plant put him in a more vulnerable position. Based on key intelligence against him and his workings, a series of government raids and seizures of his stockpiles and fields in 1988 resulted in his terrible loss. The loss of the vast expanse of the plantation fields and the stock of marijuana greatly weakened him on the financial side of things. It also reflected the loopholes in his drug operations, which hit his credibility to a great extent. The members of the Medellin Cartel, not to mention other cartels, lost trust in his abilities and standings within the enterprise, affecting his marijuana operations in the Caribbean regions.

His aggressive policies (such as the bombing of the United States Embassy, the massacre of the local Kankuama people, and attacks on the police and military bases) put him in quite a vulnerable position, cautioning the law enforcement agencies to take the drug operations of the Medellin Cartel and Gacha seriously. Before his aggressive drug trade, the drug operations were not considered serious crimes either in Colombia or in the United States, but his aggressive operations put law enforcement agencies on guard internationally. In the 1980s, as the operations of cartels became violent, the Colombian government formed a collaboration with international law enforcement agencies, including the United States DEA and CIA, to intensify their policies to track him and his cartel down as soon as possible. Gacha's failed attacks and massacre worsened the situation for him, as his drug trafficking routes would eventually be cut off.

The Colombian government, especially that of Virgilio Barco, eagerly pursued the fight against drugs so as to reduce the cases of drug trafficking. This period saw the focus shift to the war on drug cartels, with governments employing more and more power and international backup to combat the organization. As the pressure rose higher, Gacha and his cronies turned to even worse tactics in their bid to retain their control. Indeed, during a period charged with the exercise of unrivaled terrorism over competitors and state institutions, the Medellín Cartel orchestrated bombings and assassinations at the behest of Gacha. The most egregious of these was the murder of presidential candidate Luis Carlos Galán, who had not been shy in his condemnation of the drug cartels. He was killed in 1989, which was a direct provocation of the government and defined the degree of cartel power and ruthlessness.

These events were quite significant in causing cracks in the powerful position of the drug kingpin, who not only built his cocaine empire in little time but also changed the dynamics of drug operations by introducing new logistics to the world of organized crimes. It was his error of judgment or his bad luck to involve himself in high-profile incidents that drew an aggressive response from the international community, leading to unprecedented pressure to track down the drug cartels. As luck would have it, a couple of wrong decisions ignited chain reactions, leading to his imminent downfall in 1989.

The Constant Conflicts and Pressure

The primary reason for the ultimate downfall of Medellin cartel, particularly Jose Gonzalo Rodriguez Gacha, was the pressure from law enforcement agencies and the rivalries that surged with his rise. These took some time to build up, but when they reached the elastic limit, it became almost impossible for him to evade them. The pressures and the rivalries were from diverse sources ranging from crackdowns by law enforcement, conflicts with the cartel rivals, the disloyalty and betrayal from within Medellin Cartel, and the financial setback as a result of raids and the shutting down of drug stockpiles and the plantation areas.

Here's how crackdowns from diverse sources led to his final downfall:

Joint Efforts by Law Enforcement

At the peak of his career as a drug lord, Gacha became the most wanted criminal in Colombia owing to his aggressive policies and the reign of terror that seeped into the public lives of the common people. It had a multifarious effect. Firstly, it led to conflicts within the cartel, but more importantly, it made the Colombian government, as well as the United States government, take drug trafficking as a serious crime. The United States particularly put pressure on the Colombian government to increase its efforts to capture the top drug lords. His violent and high-profile criminal actions, including bombings and attacks against public institutions, public figures, and the United States embassy, made him the most wanted criminal, at the top of the ladder of the list to be dismantled. These violent attacks pushed international forces to be more vigilant and to scrutinize the situation for the crackdown. The United States went to the extent of providing financial resources to the Colombian government. Besides the financial resources, it also provided the services of its law enforcement institutions like the DEA and CIA to Colombian military units, helping them execute surveillance activities that focused on capturing Jose Gonzalo Rodriguez Gacha.

Both the Colombian law enforcement agencies as well as international agencies collectively executed numerous raids on marijuana fields, cocaine fields, refinery laboratories, and safe havens where they kept the stockpiles to catch Gacha red-handed. These law enforcement operations and raids forced him to hide and disrupt his drug smuggling routes and operations.

Failed Ventures Resulting in Financial Loss

Gacha used to cultivate cocaine and marijuana fields for processing and then finally smuggling drugs across the globe. He heavily invested in those fields and the refinery laboratories to make drug trafficking more cost-effective. Unfortunately, when law enforcement tightened its hold to check the drug operations, it did raids on the fields where he used to grow marijuana and cocaine. They even attacked the stockpile where the drugs were hidden for trafficking. The direct result of these raids and crackdowns was that Gacha lost a lot of financial resources to properly maintain his kingdom of drug trafficking.

His major setback happened when the crackdown campaign launched by the Government engulfed his marijuana fields, resulting in the seizure and destruction of huge quantities of stockpiles of drugs. His estate and the stockpiles of drugs in Colombia's Caribbean region were hit the most, making him face huge financial losses, so much so that he did not have money readily available to invest in drug operations, including cultivation and transportation.

The second reason he faced huge financial loss was his failed attempts to expand his networks in Mexico. The purpose of expansion in Mexico was to create new transportation routes and partnerships. However, the response from the Mexican drug lords was quite cold, as they had reservations regarding his violent approach towards drug operations. Because he did not receive an anticipatory positive response from the Mexican drug traffickers, financial loss was the automatic result.

Rifts From Within the Cartels

There was a time when Gacha faced plenty of rivalries and clashes from within the Medellin Cartel, weakening his power even further. It is surprising to note that most of the time, the conflicts happened due to clashes in the ideology of drug operation. His violent and intimidating policies were not well received by the leading members of the cartel, so much so that they fell out with him frequently. For example, Pablo Escobar did not approve of his decision related to bombing campaigns and assassinations. He thought that these intimidating activities attracted the attention of law enforcement agencies, who tightened their grip on drug operations even more.

Also, they resulted in outrage from the public, who subsequently clamored for the cartel to be destroyed. These issues caused friction because Gacha, instead of listening to them, was quite a headstrong leader who followed his own will, which resulted in fissures within the cartel, leading to the weakening of his position. Ultimately, he was isolated to a great extent within the enterprise.

The second source of friction was from the Cali Cartel. There was a constant rivalry between the Cali Cartel and the Medellin Cartel, which resulted in violent clashes quite frequently. These confrontations had quite an influence on the finances of the cartel, which also led to the weakening of cartel's financial resources. Also, these battles drew more attention from law enforcement to disrupt their drug operations and the violent wars, disrupting the peace of Colombia. The characterization of Gacha and the Cali Cartel is one of venomous antagonists with petulant battles, yet it is a relationship that switches between one of rivalry and a begrudging alliance. During the last of the 1980s, both cartels came under pressure from the Colombian government and international forces. This resulted in acquiring interests and temporary alliances with the intention of countering their threats. However, such alliances were marked with compromise and treachery. The war between the Medellin and Cali Cartels was never entirely shelved, and tensions remained high between the two groups. The leaders of the Cali Cartel, such as Gilberto Rodríguez Orejuela, started to position themselves strategically so that they could capitalize from the weakened Medellin Cartel. The others saw him as an opponent and didn't leave him alone, trying to take advantage of his weaknesses.

Disloyalties and Information Leaks

He also became a victim of disloyalty and betrayal even from the people he used to trust within his own network. It was hard for the leading drug lords to see him rise at a constant pace, and in such little time too. His downfall would have been postponed for at least one more decade if his allies and friends had not ratted him out to law enforcement agencies. His trusted associates, feeling threatened by his violent and ruthless methods, revealed intelligence about his whereabouts or his drug operations, allowing DEA and other law enforcement agencies to raid his safe havens, routes, estates, and stockpiles of drugs. For example, Evaristo Porras was allegedly the one responsible for providing quite sensitive information about Gacha, his operations, drug smuggling routes, and locations for targeting him effectively.

His brutal methods and volatile temper had a great role to play, as these became a prime reason for his confidants and trustworthy members to alienate him. He started shooting allies and confidants on the basis of mere suspicion or even fear, which resulted in greater isolation within the cartel. Likewise, many of his associates from the drug networks also started distancing themselves from him because they did not want to become victims of collateral damage in his violent confrontations. His isolation from outside and within the cartel became a prime reason for his diminishing power.

Hence, it was the combination of law enforcement raids, rivalries within the cartel, internal betrayals, and financial loss that led to his ultimately weakened position. His isolation and alienation also contributed a lot to the final blow that hit him hard enough to end him once and for all.

Government's Role

The other factor that led to the collapse of Gacha's empire was the direct interference of the U. S. government in the war against narcotics trafficking. The U.S. offered most of the financial support to the Colombian police force in addition to sharing information and assets intended to dismantle the cartels. This international pressure piled more operational worries on hm as well as his allies. Bureaus like the Drug Enforcement Administration (DEA) were very instrumental in identifying and pursuing drug barons. Together with the DEA activities, enhanced cooperation between the Colombian and the U.S. agencies raised the efficiency of anti-drug activities. It brought the international focus on Gacha, and it added to the various pressures he was facing.

Scrutiny and Surveillance Efforts of the Colombian Government

As the drug smuggling trade picked up its activities, widening its network and spreading its influence across the globe, the government of Colombia started taking the drug smuggling as a serious crime. A natural reaction to the worst effects of drug operations was that the government ramped up its intelligence and surveillance against the leading drug lords as well as drug cartels. Jose Gonzalo Rodriguez Gacha is one of the most influential as well as violent drug lords who attracted the attention of the Colombian government. Following are the various tactics used by the Colombian government to track him down:

Wiretapping and Interception

The leading role was played by the Colombian national police, who began intercepting the communication between the cartel members to track down their locations, routes, and logistics related to drug operations. For example, their interception was precise to the extent of having access to their phone calls, radio communications, and other means of communication with other drug lords. It was through these wiretaps that they learned about his movements and contacts.

Information Extraction Through Informants

The government of Colombia also reached out to informants and disloyal members of the cartel who were ready to rat Gacha and his cartel out. In some cases, the government paid the informants for their services, and in other cases, they were given leniency for drug operations or previous transgressions. They also infiltrated the cartels' networks, gaining an inside report about the functioning and the operations of the cartel. Many of the informants were the former allies of him who had isolated Gacha either out of fear or because of rivalries.

Collaboration With the DEA and CIA

The Colombian government was not alone in tracking down Gacha and his cartel; it was constantly assisted by the DEA as well as the CIA. Both the CIA and DEA played an instrumental role in bringing an end to the era of Jose Gonzalo Rodriguez Gacha. They also helped provide the latest technology to target him, such as satellite imagery, surveillance technology, and intelligence-gathering capabilities, which went a long way in keeping close surveillance of his movement.

Targeted Operations

The Colombian government carried out targeted operations to attack Gacha and his associates, along with drug operations, plantation fields, and refineries. For that purpose, they conducted an operation in Tolu Sucre on December 15, 1989, to apprehend Gacha. This operation was led by an efficient team selected from the National Police's elite Search Bloc. They tracked him down when he was hiding in Tolu, accompanied by his son Feddy and his bodyguards. Tolu is a secluded place in a coastal town located in the Sucre department.

It was a combined attack from the air as well as the ground, with helicopters surrounding the ranch to prevent him from escaping. At the same time, the ground forces encircled the ranch from all sides and closed in on the location. Just before he could escape from the surrounding forces in his car, he was ambushed by the police forces. It was not long when, after a chase and firefight, Gacha was finally killed by the surrounding forces along with his son and his bodyguards.

Extradition Policy and Political Pressure

The United States put a lot of pressure on the Colombian government to bring down the operations of the cartel along with its members; on top of that, it threatened the government with extradition of the cartel members to the United States. However, the extradition treaty had a benefit for the Colombian government as they could foresee their advantage in its culmination. This realization struck the government, especially after the assassinations of prominent public figures like Justice Minister Rodrigo Lara Bonilla in 1984. The treaty had a chilling effect on violent leaders like Gacha, who could foresee the intensity of the torture and punishment in the United States after the capture.

One more step that the government took to bring an end to the era of intensive drug operations was to strengthen as well as implement legal reforms in the laws against drug operations. These anti-narcotic laws allowed quicker persecutions of the drug lords, ensuring harsher penalties. These harsher penalties and anti-narcotic laws helped put additional pressure on the cartel members, disrupting their drug operations.

Public Outrage and Diplomatic Pressure

The violent tactics and drug operations, as well as the cartels' confrontations, led to a general hatred towards the drug lords, who was the mastermind behind all the bombings and attacks on public figures as well as institutions.

In this regard, the mass media came in handy in shaping public opinion against the drug lords. The Colombians accessed the mass media to project such campaigns to target the drug lords. The task was made easier when high-profile figures were assassinated in the warfare, such as the murder of presidential candidate Luis Carlos Galan and several judges, journalists, and public officials. The mass media making these assassinations a premise projected an intense hatred against the drug lords like Gacha, who were directly involved in the assassinations.

The Colombian government also sought diplomatic support of the international community in an effort to work up an international opinion against Jose Gonzalo Rodriguez Gacha. The direct result of this positively orchestrated international diplomatic response was that it acquired economic aid, military assistance, and diplomatic pressure to isolate not only the cartels but also Gacha internationally and target them more effectively.

Crackdown of Gacha's Network and Assets

The Colombian government launched various attacks on the drug networks and assets to disrupt their activities. It seized his assets and froze the funds he had accumulated after much toil. His financial and material resources included properties, ranches, and businesses. The newly implemented anti-narcotic laws helped the government confiscate Gacha's assets, disrupting his financial and funding operations.

The government also launched attacks on the supply chains by damaging his drug refinery labs, airplanes that he used for the transportation of the drugs, and other infrastructures that were quite crucial to the drug operations. Since his kingdom encompassed these assets, including the plantation fields, refineries, and trading routes, it was the most affected by these heavy wipeout operations.

The Colombian government also targeted allies, suppliers, transporters, and partners in the business of drug trafficking, damaging his position even further. They targeted the allies and the associates, particularly the paramilitary forces financed by Gacha both legally and militarily, to weaken him effectively.

Operations Against Guerrilla Forces

His links with the right-winged paramilitary groups made him more controversial and troublesome. Gacha's funded and organized paramilitary forces were there to protect him against guerrilla groups such as the Revolutionary Armed Forces of Colombia (FARC). The Colombian government used both police and military to counter guerrilla groups as well as the paramilitaries. The weakening of these groups indirectly weakened Gacha's hold. Their operations included disruption of the paramilitary alliance. It leveraged the internal conflicts between the paramilitary forces and the cartel leaders in its favor to attack his associates and alliances through a divide-and-conquer strategy.

The pressure on him had mounted to the intolerant level by the latter half of the same year, namely, the degrading of available resources in the face of its escalating and guaranteed demands. However, frequent violence, a crackdown by the government, and his rivalry with the Cali Cartel affected his operations. The government, being very determined to finish off these drug lords, has, in the recent past, initiated a sequence of operations to either arrest or neutralize some of the cartel leaders.

The Final Showdown

As indicated by constant pressures from the public, media, and international diplomats to bring an end to an abusive era of drug trafficking and cartel's violent methods, his final showdown was imminent.

Gacha understood the precariousness of his situation, so much so that he was constantly in movement to evade capture and his extradition to the United States. He was very well aware of the intense manhunt, which is why he kept hiding in unknown locations. His trick was to keep moving his residence locations, of which only a small number of allies and close associates, such as bodyguards and intimate family, were aware. Ironically, it was this constant movement from one place to another that made him more vulnerable, disturbing his communication with the drug operations of the cartel.

As has been mentioned earlier, Gacha (due to his rising power and his temper) formed rivalries with various drug lords and allies. It was these allies who became informants of law enforcement later on when they fell out with him. One such former alliance tipped the Colombian national police in December 1989 about his location; at the time, he was in hiding in the town of Tolu, Sucre, Colombia. This informant was none other than a close associate who knew the precise details of the whereabouts of Gacha. The Colombian national police, in collaboration with the DEA, was already on guard, and they instantly planned a decisive operation to hunt him down.

The Raid and Gacha's Death

As soon as the intelligence regarding the current location of Gacha reached law enforcement, a special unit was formed instantly. The members of the unit were especially taken from the national police's Search Bloc to chalk a detailed plan to attack the ranch near Tolu where he was in hiding along with his few trustworthy bodyguards and his son.

It is surprising to see the resilience and the willpower of Jose Gonzalo Rodriguez Gacha, who, even being raided by the air force as well as the ground, tried his best to escape from the attack in his convoy of vehicles. At that time, he was not all alone; his son Fredy was also accompanying him with several bodyguards. As luck would have it, he was intercepted by the police forces, who were quick enough to surround the area with aerial forces as well as ground fleet to hunt him down. It was amidst gunfire and a wild chase that he was finally shot down with his apparently reliant squad.

Securing the Scene

Right after the attack on Gacha's ranch near Tolu, when he was finally hunted down after a lot of chasing and gunfights, the area was secured from all sides. The police officers who killed him approached the vehicles and confirmed his death. They identified his body from his facial features. However, he had various injuries on his face, so much so that it was a little difficult to recognize him due to gunshot wounds. As soon as the approaching police officers confirmed his death, they took steps to let the world know about this drastic development. The media, along with the Colombian officials, were the first to be informed about the news.

Public Announcement and Media Coverage

The Colombian government quickly announced the death of José Gonzalo Rodríguez Gacha, celebrating it as a major victory in the fight against the Medellín Cartel. The media covered the event extensively, showing images of Gacha's bullet-riddled body and the scene of the confrontation. This news was welcomed by many Colombians, who saw it as a sign that the government was taking decisive action against the cartels.

The Aftermath of Gacha's Death

Despite an overall dislike for Gacha, his death was a huge blow to the existence of the Medellin Cartel and its leaders. The demise of one of the most forceful and invincible leaders not only weakened the Medellin Cartel and its drug operations but also conveyed the potential of the Colombian government in its commitment to dismantling the cartel by any means necessary. Although Pablo Escobar continued leading the Medellin Cartel's operations, it lost its previous might, geographical control, and influence. It also lost its operational capabilities, shattering the myth of its invincibility and helplessness of the Colombian government. It was indeed a turning event for the Colombian government, which successfully demonstrated its effectiveness in collaboration with law enforcement and military actions.

The violent end to José Rodríguez Gacha's existence happened during the Christmas season, on December 15, 1989. This encounter took place at a time when he was becoming more and more exposed and the government and international organizations accelerated their attempts to arrest him. Famous for his violent and rough behavior, was finally traced and eliminated in a gun battle. His death was a considerable shift in the war against drug trafficking in Colombia.

CHAPTER 6
THE AFTER-EFFECTS OF RODRÍGUEZ GACHA - LEGACY AND IMPACT OF HIS DEATH

On December 15, 1989, the assassination of Jose Gonzalo Rodriguez Gacha at the hands of the Colombian National Police marked the end of an era. It proved to be a turning point for the Medellin Cartel enterprise because he was one of the top leaders of the cartel. After all, he was the mastermind behind handling large-scale cocaine shipments. He also diligently established the trafficking routes, which were protected by paramilitary forces to ensure the smooth conduction of the drug operations. It would not be an exaggeration to claim that the death of Jose Gacha shot the cartel, but equally true is the fact the impact was gradual, dismantling the cartel gradually. The effect of his death could be divided into three parts, beginning with the immediate effect of his death on the cartel.

Prompt Effect of Gacha's Death

He was one of the top leaders of the cartel. Right after death, the cartel kept on functioning under the leadership of Pablo Escobar along with the Ochoa brothers. The immediate impact of his absence was that Pablo tightened his grip on the organization, taking a much more dominating role than he had during his life. However, the cartel was not as strong as it was before his death as it lost important networks, connections, and paramilitary forces, which worked like a bloodline for the smooth and protective operations of drug plantations, processing, and transportation.

More Aggressive Strategy Against the Government

It is quite ironic to note that Escobar had always been against the aggressive policies and drug trade methods of Gacha, but when he was killed and the major responsibility of the cartel fell upon the shoulders of Escobar, he resorted to even more aggressive methods. Intensifying the aggressive campaign of the cartel, he was responsible for the killings of high-profile figures, including politicians, judges, police officers, and journalists. In order to regain the weakening position of the Medellin Cartel, he orchestrated the bombing incident that attacked Avianca Flight 203 in November 1989, which resulted in the killing of over 100 people (Shiffman, 2020).

War With the Colombian Government

The Colombian government, feeling more confident and gaining better credibility, escalated its efforts to crack down on the cartel with the unwavering support of the United States. The collaboration between the Drug Enforcement Administration and the Colombian law enforcement agencies became more serious and effective, so much so that the Colombian government formulated a Special Search Bloc designated to dismantle Pablo Escobar and other leaders of the cartel. The support of the United States included intelligence sharing, provision of hi-tech resources, and training to the Colombian law enforcement agencies to make the efforts more effective.

Fragmentation of the Cartel

Gacha's death also caused internal conflicts among the members, particularly the top leaders of the Medellín Cartel. Some of its leading members, who found his strategies questionable, also began to question Escobar's leadership. They found his strategies increasingly erratic and aggressive. They also determined that his aggressive, erratic, and violent methods attracted more intense scrutiny from law enforcement and international authorities. For example, the Ochoa brothers were more inclined towards negotiations to avoid extradition and to safeguard their wealth and families. In contrast, Escobar remained more rigid, refusing to make any compromises with the government.

Rise of Los Pepes

The death of Gacha in December 1989 and the rise of Pablo as a leader made many members of the Medellin Cartel disillusioned and dissatisfied with the functioning of the cartel. As a result, they formed a new alliance that consisted of enemies of Escobar as well as members of the Cali Cartel. It is quite interesting that the newly formed group also had members from paramilitary groups and the Colombian Government. Together, all the aforementioned members contributed to creating a vigilante group afresh. The group was named "Los Pepes," meaning people persecuted by Pablo Escobar. The purpose of the Los Pepes was to start a campaign of violence and intimidation against Escobar's associates, lawyers, and family members. As a counteraction, they ran a series of bombings and assassinations that had one unified goal: to cripple Escobar's network of support.

Allegedly, it received support from the Colombian Government and international law enforcement agencies, including the DEA. The resources and intelligence were used by Los Pepes with the aim of targeting anyone connected to Escobar. Creating an intimidating climate within the Medellín Cartel influenced and forced many of its members to betray Pablo Escobar and ally with authorities or simply hide themselves from the massacre. The group's activities significantly diminished Escobar's organization by gradually disrupting its support base and logistics.

Hard Hit to Escobar's Power and the Medellín Cartel

From late 1992 to 1993, the grip around Escobar tightened. Many of his closest allies had turned disloyal; a number of them were targeted, arrested, or even killed. As such he became all very vulnerable all of a sudden. Just like Gacha was tracked down in his ranch in Tolu, the Colombian National Police (with the assistance of the United States intelligence and surveillance technology) discovered the whereabouts of Escobar in a safe house in Medellín. On December 2, 1993, the Colombian police tracked and killed Escobar in a shootout on the rooftop. It was with his death that the Medellín Cartel experienced the end of an influential era. Essentially, its standing as a dominant force in international cocaine operations had all but perished.

With the death of Escobar, the Medellín Cartel shattered and lost its resilience, with fragments either being adopted by other criminal organizations or disappearing entirely. As far as the fate of the Ochoa brothers is concerned, they too gave in eventually to the authorities, with many other mid to low-level drug dealers hunted down. The deaths of Gacha and Escobar created a leadership vacuum, which led to the failure of the cartel's infrastructure, thus leaving a void in Colombia's drug trade.

Rise of the Cali Cartel

As soon as the Medellín Cartel weakened and fragmented, the rise of the Cali Cartel was a natural development. The prominence in organized crime was taken over by the Rodríguez Orejuela brothers, who emerged as the new as new Colombian drug lords in the cocaine trade. The Cali Cartel, learning from the experiences and the fatal end of the Medellin Cartel, kept a more low-profile approach. They relied more on using bribery and corruption, and they avoided outright violence to deescalate the situation created by the violent approach of Jose Gacha and later on by Pablo Escobar. The strategy allowed them to operate for a longer period. The peaceful strategy influenced and encouraged other smaller cartels and organized crime groups to jump into the drug trafficking landscape, making the business more fragmented in Colombia.

Long-Term Impact

It is quite noteworthy to notice that the emergence of fragmented criminal groups dealing in the drug trade and the peaceful conduction of the operations reduced the violence in Colombia; however, the drug trade operations continued as per the routine. It evolved with the changing dynamics of the criminal world and with different cartels and groups taking control. The power shift was responsible for the rise of other criminal organizations like the Norte del Valle Cartel, and paramilitary groups and guerrilla movements like the FARC became active in the drug trade.

The Medellín Cartel's story underscores the complexities and challenges in the global fight against drug trafficking. One cannot help but ignore the collateral damage caused by the violence and firefights amid law enforcement and drug trafficking. There started widespread violence, corruption, and socio-political instability due to such criminal organizations' dominance in the country.

Changes in the Drug Trade

The changes that followed were so huge not only in Colombia but also in the international arena. There was a drastic shift in how the emerging drug dealers conducted cocaine trafficking operations. Instead of focusing on the violence and running huge cartels and operations, they concentrated the drug operations on a small scale. Here is how the key changes that were experienced by the drug trade world after the death of Gacha and the collapse of the Medellín Cartel:

Shift of Power

The dominant cocaine trafficking organization in Colombia was taken over by the Rodríguez Orejuela brothers, Gilberto and Miguel. Similar to the Cali Cartel, they permanently displaced the Medellín Cartel by employing low-profile strategies that relied on bribes and trickery.

Cali Cartel tricked law enforcement agencies and the government with the use of bribery and corruption. They managed their earnings with much more sophisticated money laundering techniques to convert the black money into white and manage its operations. The practice of bribing law enforcement officials, judges, and politicians allowed the Cali Cartel to prolong as well as expand its influence. Through peaceful practices, the deviated law enforcement agencies were prevented from conducting any strict crackdown operations on them. Gradually, through this peaceful technique, the Cali Cartel developed a global distribution network with strong associations and networks in Europe, including in Spain. It escalated its market share in the United States by diversifying into other criminal enterprises that were responsible for the kidnapping, extortion, and smuggling of contraband goods.

Decentralization of Drug Trafficking

The decline of the Medellín Cartel initiated the fragmentation of the cocaine trade, leading to its operation by smaller criminal groups. This decline created a vacuum in the drug trade, which was filled by organizations such as the Norte del Valle Cartel, Los Rastrojos, Los Urabeños (also known as Clan del Golfo), and other criminal groups. Although these groups were not as unified or as expansive as the Medellin Cartel in their drug activities, they conducted a more fragmented drug trade landscape effectively. Smaller cartels and groups focused more on establishing dominance over small and specific territories and cocaine plantation regions. The conflicts and alliances were of a localized nature; they took place due to claims of having control over coca-growing areas, refinery laboratories, and smuggling routes.

Emergence of New Alliances and Shifts in Drug Trafficking Routes

The old dynamics of drug trafficking also underwent a change, including changes in drug trafficking routes and alliances between cartels; the change happened both within Colombia and internationally. The new era demanded the diversification of trafficking routes because old routes were under severe surveillance by law enforcement agencies. For example, the traditional routes of the Caribbean and South Florida were under close observation to check the drug activities. As a result, traffickers began to diversify their routes by creating new ones through Central America and Mexico. They also shifted the aerial and the water routes to an increased use of overland routes. More sophisticated methods, such as semi-submersible submarines and drones, were also utilized to evade disruption.

The Role of Nonstate Actors

Different nonstate forces, including paramilitary groups and guerrilla organizations, actively participated in the drug trade. The emergence and involvement of paramilitary and guerrillas like AUC and FARC also started dominating drug operations. The paramilitary forces started investing in drug operations to engage in drug trafficking because they needed the money to operate counterinsurgency operations. The FARC fulfilled its need for money by taxing the coca growers and by directly controlling their own drug production and trafficking networks. This involvement of the nonstate actors in furthering the drug operations led to a further blurring of lines between political conflict and organized crime in Colombia.

Technological Advancements and Drug Smuggling

Traffickers changed the traditional methods with new technologies and innovative smuggling techniques to adjust to the changing landscape of drug operations. The new drug smugglers and the drug lords adopted new and improved transportation methods. They started using more advanced methods for the transportation of cocaine, such as semi-submersible submarines, tunnels, light aircraft, and drones. This shift in the selection of the mode of transportation also provided them with an opportunity to bypass traditional checkpoints and detection methods more effectively.

In the later years, drug trafficking organizations were smart enough to start experimenting with digital currencies and encrypted communication platforms to conduct monetary transactions and to do money laundering effectively. This adaptation of cryptocurrency, as well as innovative digital tools, has made it more challenging for the authorities to track the financial flows associated with the drug trade.

International Cooperation in Law Enforcement

The direct result of these developments was that international law enforcement agencies became more active in shutting down what was left of the Medellin Cartel. The United States played a great role in providing military aid, training, and intelligence to Colombia under the umbrella of projects like "Plan Colombia." The purpose was to help combat drug trafficking and related violence, which was a direct result of the drug mafia. This cooperation led to the capture or killing of several top drug lords, disrupting the activities of many smaller cartels. A greater focus on extradition to the United States also sped up the dismantling of the drug lords one after another.

Feeling accomplished after the fall of Gacha and his cartel, law enforcement agencies around the world began employing more advanced surveillance techniques, financial investigations, and the use of informants to dismantle the activities of drug trafficking. This approach was bent upon wiping out entire networks rather than just targeting individual drug lords.

Impact on Colombian Society and Politics

The end of Gacha's empire had a profound effect on Colombian society and politics as a whole. A conspicuous shift in public perception regarding the drug lord, cartels' operations, and law enforcement agencies was observed. There was a stronger desire for peace and stability, as the people had had enough of the years of violence and terror that ensued because of the cartel's operations. This sentiment of positivism also contributed to political efforts toward peace negotiations with other armed groups like the FARC.

However, the new nuances attached to drug trafficking have raised concerns regarding corruption and governance challenges. The drug trade, despite being less violent lately, has continued to have a corrosive effect on Colombian governance. The ongoing infiltration of drug money in the political sphere has played a significant role in corrupting the judiciary and law enforcement. With the efforts of the Colombian government, some progress has been made, but corruption still remains a significant challenge contributing to the erosion of society.

Resilience of the Cocaine Trade

Despite the demise of the Medellín Cartel, the cocaine trade has proven remarkably resilient to date with different key players in the world of organized crime. It is no wonder that coca cultivation in Colombia has remained high due to ongoing demand. There are still favorable growing conditions and economic incentives for local farmers who contribute a lot to furthering the drug trade. Even with aggressive eradication efforts pursued by the Colombian government in collaboration with international law enforcement agencies, the cultivation of marijuana and cocaine has persisted. That is because of an increased global demand and the profitability of cocaine. With the fragmented drug trade and peaceful conduction of drug operations, the cocaine trade became more globalized, with new markets emerging in Europe, Asia, and Africa. The drug traffickers are smart enough to leverage the changes in law enforcement tactics, and they continue to innovate, making the global fight against cocaine trafficking increasingly complex and difficult to achieve.

A significant transformation has taken place in the drug trade world. While the cartel's demise signified the end of an era that was defined by the extreme violence and terror tactics of Medellín, it also led to the rise of new formations, alliances, and involvement of nonstate actors who made incredible efforts to change the trafficking routes, incur technological advancements, and create a more fragmented and decentralized drug trade landscape. Despite the efforts of law enforcement and governments worldwide, the cocaine trade adapted, evolved, and continued to thrive in new forms, presenting ongoing challenges for global counter-narcotics efforts.

New Law Enforcement Strategies After Jose Gacha's Death

Law enforcement strategies in Colombia became more committed to disrupting the dominance of drug cartels and dismantling the influence of organized crime. Here is how the key law enforcement strategies and changes were implemented after the death of Jose Gacha to tighten the noose around the drug operations:

Improved Cooperation Between Colombia and the United States

The credibility of the Colombian government's commitment to disrupt the drug operations improved after eliminating Gacha's empire. It also indicated the effectiveness of international cooperation in combating drug trafficking. In the years following, Colombia and the United States strengthened their ties and strategic relations. This led to stronger collaboration on the sharing of intelligence, better effectiveness of joint operations, and the furthering of extradition agreements. The support of the United States escalated as they provided more financial aid, equipment, and training for Colombian law enforcement and military personnel to target drug cartels more effectively.

Incorporation of New Legal Frameworks and Extradition Policies

Gacha's death led to a call for the revision of laws and constitutional provisions. The new laws were made to facilitate the extradition of drug traffickers to the United States. At the onset, it became quite a controversial strategy, but if one digs deeper, it was a more effective strategy, as it meant to facilitate the targeting of cartel members. It also laid the groundwork for the drug lords to face harsher penalties in U.S. courts. The new laws also encompassed checking money laundering and asset forfeiture, enabling authorities to hold or freeze the assets of drug traffickers and target their financial networks.

Formation of Anti-Drug Units

Colombia escalated the use of specialized anti-narcotics units and formed new military and paramilitary groups that were focused specifically on checking drug trafficking operations. With the help of new laws and their implementation, these units conducted high-profile raids, operations, and intelligence missions that were targeted to break the influence of the cartels.

Strengthening of Local Law Enforcement and Intelligence Capabilities

Colombian law enforcement and military forces made serious efforts to improve their intelligence capabilities, surveillance, and technology to target and seize drug traffickers effectively. Because of corruption via bribery and the inclusion of nonstate actors into the drug operations, efforts were also made to reduce corruption within local law enforcement, as it had become a significant challenge in combating drug trafficking at the time.

Focused Approach to Hunt Down Cali Cartel and Other Successors

Other emerging drug lords, small organizations, and paramilitary forces became a prime focus. The main target became the other emerging cartels, such as the Cali Cartel. The Cali Cartel operated with a different strategy, favoring bribery and corruption over outright violence. This posed new challenges for law enforcement to introduce a new set of laws that could deal with the situation as destructive as violence.

Shift Toward Criminal Justice Reform and Human Rights

The Medellin Cartel's era ended in violence and aggression, and after the height of violence in the late 1980s and early 1990s, it created a growing recognition of the need for broader criminal justice reforms and respect for human rights in law enforcement operations. This was meant to discourage the transgressors of the law. The Colombian government tried to balance aggressive anti-drug measures with reforms aimed at addressing the underlying social and economic issues that fueled drug trafficking. The purpose of these strategies was to take up a more comprehensive approach to combatting drug trafficking and organized crime in Colombia. At the same time, these strategies were meant to set the stage for later efforts to address the complex issues surrounding the drug trade. The purposes also included peace processes with guerrilla groups and initiatives to provide alternative livelihoods for communities involved in drug cultivation.

Impact on Global Drug Policy

The death of José Gonzalo Rodríguez Gacha also had an important effect on global drug policy. It influenced the way countries approached the battle against drug smuggling, which led to cooperation at the international level in structuring policies to combat organized crime. Here's an overview of important consequences:

A Trendsetter for International Cooperation

The world witnessed a strengthened U.S.-Colombia Alliance. As a result of a joint operation by Colombian police, the DEA highlighted the importance of international collaboration. Due to increased credibility in the Colombian government, the United States escalated its support for Colombia with more financial aid, intelligence sharing, and training to combat drug cartels. This set a precedent for other countries to cooperate closely with the U.S. on anti-drug initiatives. Colombia became more active in forming regional partnerships with other Latin American countries to combat drug trafficking. This included intelligence sharing and joint operations to address the transnational nature of the drug trade.

Shift in Focus to Cartel Leadership

The Colombian government, in alliance with international law enforcement agencies, adopted the "Kingpin Strategy". Later, other cartel leaders encouraged the U.S. and other countries to adopt a "Kingpin Strategy," which focused more on targeting the top leadership of drug cartels instead of targeting the cartel as a whole. This approach aimed to dismantle cartels by capturing or killing their leaders, a strategy that was later employed against other drug lords like Pablo Escobar and, much later, Joaquín "El Chapo" Guzmán.

With the removal of Gacha and other Medellín Cartel leaders, the global drug policy saw an increased emphasis on targeting specific organizations.

Development of New Legal Frameworks and Extradition Treaties

The success of collaborative efforts between Colombia and the U.S. increased support for extradition treaties. Countries began to revise their legal frameworks to allow the extradition of drug traffickers, facilitating their prosecution in jurisdictions with tougher penalties. Colombia, for instance, strengthened its extradition policies despite internal opposition. Many nations adopted stronger legal measures to confiscate the assets of drug traffickers and implement anti-money laundering laws, recognizing the effectiveness of these approaches in weakening the financial power of cartels.

Reevaluation of Militarized Approaches

The death of key cartel leaders reaffirmed the effectiveness of using military force and special operations to combat drug trafficking by targeting top leadership. This resulted in increased militarization of the drug war in Colombia and later in Mexico, as both countries deployed military units in anti-drug operations. However, this approach led to heightened aggression and human rights abuses, drawing criticism from organizations advocating for human rights and prompting calls for a reevaluation of global drug policy. It became clear that a militaristic strategy alone could not address the socio-economic factors driving the drug trade.

Increased Focus on Narco-terrorism

Anti-narcotic operations against Gacha led to a global push to perceive and treat drug cartels, not just as criminal enterprises but also as terrorist organizations, influencing international policies to combat "narco-terrorism." The U.S., in particular, began treating drug trafficking as a national security issue, increasing the involvement of agencies like the DEA, FBI, and the Department of Defense.

Shift Towards Alternative Development Programs

As the militarized approach led to some short-term successes and long-term challenges, there was an increased focus on alternative development programs. These programs aimed to provide legal, economic opportunities to farmers involved in coca cultivation, recognizing that long-term solutions to drug trafficking required addressing underlying socio-economic issues. The authorities around the world felt a need to create circumstances where people like Gacha, with humble backgrounds but bigger dreams, could succeed in life without falling victim to the criminal world.

Impact on Drug Policy

Policymakers worldwide recognized that dismantling drug cartels required multifaceted strategies that combined law enforcement, judicial reform, and social and economic development. The ongoing challenges in combating drug trafficking contributed to debates about alternative approaches, including the decriminalization and legalization of certain drugs. This debate has gained traction in various countries as a response to the high costs and limited success of traditional drug war tactics.

Recognition of the Need for Comprehensive Strategies

Global drug policy began to incorporate the public health approach even more, as governments recognized that addiction and drug abuse are public health issues rather than purely criminal matters. This shift led to policies focused on harm reduction, education, and treatment programs.

The death of José Gacha catalyzed significant changes in global drug policy, leading to increased international cooperation, new legal frameworks, and both militarized and developmental approaches to tackling drug trafficking. While aggressive law enforcement strategies have been found to be effective, governments around the world are also aware of the limitations of these approaches and the need for more comprehensive, balanced policies in order to address the broader socio-economic and public health dimensions of the drug trade.

CONCLUSION

The era of Medellin Cartel stands as the most conspicuous period in the history of drug trafficking in Colombia.

Jose Gacha, who had a simple dream of living a better life with better resources at his disposal, left his studies. Little did he know that as soon as he left his studies, the world of organized crime would become his fate. But his life as a drug lord reflects not only flaws in his own personality for choosing the world of crime but also that of the system of the Colombian state. When he started working as a laborer in the emerald mines, his intent was just to earn money to support his family. Ironically, it proved to be his first exposure to the world of crime, where different emerald traders were involved in the illicit emerald trade. There was a stark contrast between the income he earned after a month's toil and the large sums of money that he could observe smugglers making. The latter swayed his heart towards the illicit trade of the stone.

His humble background and poor, innocent family convey to us that criminals do not necessarily have anything remarkable in their genes; it is the desire to break the shackles of oppression and seek better opportunities that lead individuals astray sometimes. It is equally true that he was a man of abilities; it was thanks to his strategic prowess, intelligence, and social skills that he progressed so fast and ended up ruling the world of organized crime in a matter of years, filling his allies and the formidable leaders of cartels in envy.

Hence, it is only right to say that José Rodríguez Gacha's death brought about a leadership crisis in the Medellín Cartel. Aside from being an influential commander, was also a mastermind behind the drug business as well as the cartel's drug maker and banker. His disappearance created a serious space that was only possible to be filled to a certain extent. There was a major problem with the internal leadership of the Medellín Cartel in that there was increased instability. The remaining leaders of the cartel (mainly Pablo Escobar) were faced with the immediate challenges of asserting dominance over the other factions and firmly controlling the activities of the cartel. Division of authority made the cartel ungainly and eroded the cartel's capacity to coordinate extensive narcotic trafficking plans. His death also took the existing rivalry within the cartel into a new level. The Medellín Cartel was already dealing with internal conflict as well as rivalry between different factions.

Whereas Gacha managed to mediate such tensions when he was alive, these rivalries further escalated after his death, resulting in internal loyalties and power struggles. This led to a period of destabilization in the cartel due to a lack of focus, which came from having no direct figurehead, and this led to factions within the cartel rising up to kill one another. This internal conflict grew worse due to the ongoing war with the rival cartels, especially the Cali Cartel. The control of the territories once under his jurisdiction led to increased attacks and infiltration by the competitors of the Medellín Cartel. The Cali Cartel, especially, was quick to take advantage of the decline of the Medellín Cartel, increasing efforts to destabilize and eliminate his men from drug smuggling routes that were earlier under their control.

Having eliminated one of the cartel's leaders, the Colombian government increased its efforts against the Medellín Cartel. The shooting death of Gacha came as a morale booster for the police, who hailed the success as a victory against the cartel. Since the cartel was weakened, the government (with the assistance of international agencies like the DEA) intensified efforts to apprehend the other culprits and confiscate their property.

This external pressure was exacerbated by the increase in governmental pressure, which in turn worsened the availability of resources and efficiency of the cartel. The Medellín Cartel was experiencing raids, arrests, and seizures of its assets more often. That was because individuals noted the activities of law enforcement and thus put pressure on the cartel and its vast systems of drug dealing and money laundering.

Some of the changes that were inevitable within Medellin Cartel due to the increased pressure and internal conflict are as follows:

The cartel started to change the ways of working, moving to the less obvious and less formal distribution of drugs. This was done through the increased use of a number of loose, less centralized networks more than attempting to have a big, obvious structure.

Despite these adjustments, the power and influence of the cartel started declining. Subsequent to the demise of Gacha, together with internal conflict and outside forces, the cartel became less successful at enforcing its authority and domination over sources of drug distribution. Similar to the first concern, the Medellin Cartel's cocaine market monopoly was being threatened by piratical organizations and a crackdown on the narcotics business.

The weakening of the cartel, which was heightened by the assassinations of Gacha less than four years after Jorge Ochoa was captured by Spanish police in November 1984, had long-term impacts on the drug business. This change in the cartel was estimated to have changed some of the power balance within the drug trafficking business. The Cali Cartel rose to power and took over, focusing on traffic routes and taking over from the Medellín Cartel. The cooperation between Colombian legislation and foreign organizations demonstrated how effectively large criminal bands and global narcotic trafficking networks could be eliminated.

The effect of losing José Rodríguez Gacha left a tremendous blow on the Medellín Cartel. It created a power vacuum, internal strife, government pressure that went up, and strategic shifts that contributed greatly to the cartel's decline. The related implications were a restructuring of the drug organizations and the display of cooperative international police capabilities. His death shows that crime and crime organizations are not stagnant but are ever-evolving and thus are a continual problem.

After his death, the fighting forces and other law enforcement organizations (those of Colombian origin and those international) also changed their tactics. This success in targeting Gacha raised the morale of the authorities, especially in the campaigns against drug traffickers, and drove them to become more forceful and perhaps more systematic. Full cooperation was demonstrated as governments strengthened partnerships, especially between Colombia's security forces and the U.S. DEA, in terms of sharing intelligence and operations.

The emphasis was placed not only on the identification and neutralization of drug cartels' chiefs and their associates but also on the discrediting and disabling of their activities and supporting structures. This consisted of attacks on the monetary systems, interruptions in the flow of goods and services, and the act of promoting technological interventions in surveillance and detection processes.

However, Gacha's demise also emphasized that there were still problems in drug policy. Though several large cartel structures disintegrated in the course of combating, small and more mobile crime syndicates continued to show the dynamism that characterized drug trafficking organizations. These new networks, which were relatively low-profile as compared to the traditional ones, presented emerging targets to the police and, therefore, a new set of methodologies to develop on a continual basis.

As we reflect on the life and times of José Rodríguez Gacha, it's clear that his story is entwined with the deeper problems that Colombia faces. Journey from small beginnings to becoming a drug lord tells us about the tough conditions that can push people towards the drug trade. It sheds light on how corruption can spread, and it shows the kind of violence that comes with the drug business.

When he died, it did shake up the Medellín Cartel but it didn't stop the drug trade altogether. Instead, what we saw was the rise of smaller, highly elusive drug groups that could quickly change their ways to avoid the police. These groups have kept the drug business going, showing just how tough the problem is to solve.

This story is a reminder that, when we fight the drug trade, we need to think about more than just catching the big names. His life suggests that we need to look at the bigger picture, to prevent the conditions that lead to drug trafficking in the first place.

As we come to the end of this story, we understand that time and the influence he had through the Medellín Cartel mark an important chapter in the fight against drugs. After he was gone, the battle against drug trafficking didn't end—it just changed. It continues to be a challenge for Colombia and the world, requiring us to stay alert, to keep improving, and most importantly, to tackle the issue from all sides. It's a fight that keeps evolving, asking us to be as flexible and creative in our approaches as the traffickers we're trying to stop.

In conclusion, the death of José Gonzalo Rodríguez Gacha had far-reaching consequences for Colombian society and the global war on drugs. His demise led to a change in terms of the approaches used and paved the way for wider, more integrated, and increasingly internationalized efforts to counter drug trafficking. Despite work being done in this fight, one will notice that challenges persist, hence the need for sustained counters and approaches that entail the use of enforcement, economic disruption, and public health.

REFERENCES

BrainyQuote. (n.d.). *Behind every great fortune lies a great crime.* https://www.goodreads.com/quotes/863792-behind-every-successful-fortune-there-is-a-crime

Brazeal, B. (2014). The history of emerald mining in Colombia: An examination of Spanish-language sources. *The Extractive Industries and Society, 1*(2), 273–283. https://doi.org/10.1016/j.exis.2014.08.006

Gelber, H. (2006). *China as "victim"? The Opium War that wasn't.* Center for European Studies. https://ces.fas.harvard.edu/uploads/files/Working-Papers-Archives/CES_WP136.pdf

Long, W. R. (1989, December 7). Bogota blast kills 45; drug kingpins blamed: Colombia: Bus bomb rips through the headquarters of the police intelligence agency. 400 are injured. *Los Angeles Times.* https://www.latimes.com/archives/la-xpm-1989-12-07-mn-253-story.html

Shiffman, G. M. (2020, January 10). *The economics of violence: How behavioral science can transform our view of crime, insurgency, and terrorism.* Cambridge University Press.

Shirk, D., & Wallman, J. (2015). Understanding Mexico's drug violence. *The Journal of Conflict Resolution, 59*(8), 1348–1376. https://www.jstor.org/stable/24546346

Tellez, J. C. (2018, November 5). Urban development in Bogotá: The metro case of study. In Y. Ergen (Ed.), *An overview of urban and regional planning.* IntechOpen.
https://www.intechopen.com/chapters/63593

U.S. Department of Justice. (1994). *Fact sheet: drug-related crime.* Office of Justice Programs.
https://bjs.ojp.gov/content/pub/pdf/DRRC.PDF

United Nations Office on Drugs and Crime. (2017). *Handbook on children recruited and exploited by terrorist and violent extremist groups: The role of the justice system.*
https://www.unodc.org/documents/justice-and-prison-reform/Child-Victims/Handbook on Children Recruited and Exploited by Terrorist and Violent Extremist Groups the Role of the Justice System.E.pdf

www.ingramcontent.com/pod-product-compliance
Lightning Source LLC
Chambersburg PA
CBHW072100110526
44590CB00018B/3253